Two Captains from Carolina

C. S. Steamer Fl

Florida   Capt J N Maffitt

MOSES GRANDY,

JOHN NEWLAND MAFFITT,

AND THE COMING OF

THE CIVIL WAR

A Nonfiction Novel by

Bland Simpson

Two Captains from Carolina

For Ann and Doug

Two Sailors in Beaufort.
With warmest wishes
and great friendship.

Bland Simpson

THE UNIVERSITY OF

NORTH CAROLINA PRESS

CHAPEL HILL

This book was published with the assistance of the William R. Kenan Jr. Fund of the University of North Carolina Press.

© 2012 Bland Simpson

Designed by Richard Hendel
Set in Miller, Giza, and Sentinel types   .
by Tseng Information Systems, Inc.

The paper in this book meets the guidelines for permanence and durability of the Committee on Production Guidelines for Book Longevity of the Council on Library Resources.

The University of North Carolina Press has been a member of the Green Press Initiative since 2003.

Library of Congress Cataloging-in-Publication Data
Simpson, Bland.
Two captains from Carolina : Moses Grandy, John Newland Maffitt, and the coming of the Civil War : a nonfiction novel / by Bland Simpson.
p. cm.
Includes bibliographical references.
ISBN 978-0-8078-3585-2 (cloth : alk. paper)
1. Grandy, Moses, b. 1786? 2. Maffitt, John Newland, 1819–1886. 3. Ship captains—North Carolina—Biography. 4. African Americans—North Carolina—Biography. 5. Irish Americans—North Carolina—Biography. 6. Seafaring life—North Carolina—History—19th century. 7. North Carolina—History—1775–1865. 8. North Carolina—Biography. I. Title.
VK139S53 2012
387.5092'2756—dc23   2012010940
[B]

16 15 14 13 12   5 4 3 2 1

For
Jack Herrick,
David Perry,
and
Frank Queen

Scientia Navalis Ventorum Marisque Dominatrix.
[Naval knowledge holds dominion over the powers
of wind and sea.]
—Frontispiece legend, David Steel, *The Elements and
Practice of Rigging and Seamanship* (1794)

The wind goeth toward the south, and turneth about
unto the north; it whirleth about continually, and the
wind returneth again according to his circuits.
—Ecclesiastes 1:6

And this ship was the latest of them all upon the
timeless seas. She set a day, and fixed a mark on history.
She was the child of all other ships that had made their
dots of time and that had brought small, vivid men and
all their history upon the water.
—Thomas Wolfe, *The Web and the Rock* (1939)

Contents

Illustrations

Eastern North Carolina, mid-nineteenth century

Two Captains

Two men rise from the North Carolina lowlands and find
their separate ways into the nineteenth-century maritime
world. The wind that blows and the ship that goes carry them
both, though at different times and well apart, to Norfolk, to
Philadelphia, to Boston and New York, to the Caribbean and
Mediterranean Seas. One is an African American born a slave
in northeastern North Carolina, the other an Irish American
born at sea in the North Atlantic, and both prove to be men of
great skill on many waters, men of much courage and bearing,
accomplished mariners, captains. Between them, their lives fall
across the first century of the Republic, and their tales are those
of illimitable, striving human spirit and also of human bondage
and destruction and the great divide that nearly sundered a
nation. Their fates could hardly have differed more.

Two Captains from Carolina

C. S. Steamer P

Grandy,
Early 1800s – Circa 1820

Pasquotank River, North Carolina

EARLY 1800S

For twelve thousand years, the dark Pasquotank River had snaked down out of the Great Dismal Swamp, its path so serpentine and narrow that white men and black called its upper reaches the same thing the Algonquians had called them for ten generations before, which in the English tongue was "Moccasin Track."

The tall young man in charge of poling and sculling and cabling the ferry-flat across this swamp river at Sawyer's Ferry in northeastern North Carolina was a hired-out Negro slave, who at fifteen years of age had already done and known things that would have thrown another man's world off its axis. From the time he was ten, he had been hired out by his owner James Grandy, with whom the slave had grown up playing and who inherited and now owned him and rented him out to work for other masters: first for a man named Kemp; then for Jemmy Coates, who whipped him with a sapling till its tip broke off in his side, and all for not hilling corn the way old Jemmy wished it done; and now for Enoch Sawyer, the collector of customs, who also owned thousands of acres in Camden and Pasquotank Counties (lands in territory called the Body, in Cowper's Trace, in the Desert Swamp) yet fed the young man so poorly that he found cornhusks and ground them into flour for whatever strength he could get from it.

Camden was his home, and for three years on Sawyer's Ferry he plied the Pasquotank River from Enoch Sawyer's plantation house on the Camden County side over to just above Knobbs Creek on the Pasquotank County side. He bathed in swamp water when he bathed at all, and in wintertime dawnings he warmed

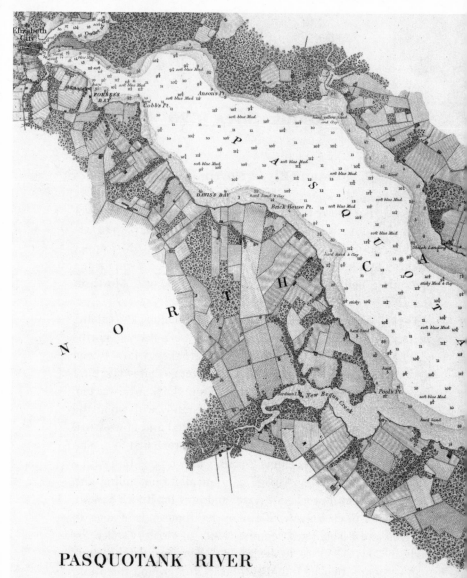

PASQUOTANK RIVER

From a Trigonometrical Survey

under the direction of A.D.BACHE Superintendent of the

SURVEY OF THE COAST OF THE UNITED STATES

Triangulation by W.M.BOYCE and J.C.NEILSON Assistants

Topography by J.C.NEILSON Assistant

Hydrography by the party

under the command of W.P.Mc.ARTHUR Lieutenant U.S.Navy

Published in 1850.

Scale 40000

Verified by
A.A.Humphreys Capt.Topl. Engrs.& Assistant.

*Pasquotank River, from the Narrows at
Elizabeth City to Albemarle Sound*

SAILING DIRECTIONS.

The Bar making off from Wades Pt. to the Light Boat in the mouth of the River forms the only obstruction to navigation. Vessels bound up the River drawing 7½ feet and upwards should pass to the Eastward of the Light Boat. When up with and near it, steer N.N.W. until Pocoson Point bears due East; then steer N.W. ¼ N. until Brick House Point bears due West; then keep in the middle of the channel, giving Cobb's Point a berth to avoid the short Bar extending in a N.E. direction from that Point.

Any part of the River inside of the Bar is a good harbor.

The Courses and Bearings are Magnetic and the Distances in Nautical miles. The Soundings are expressed in feet and show the depth at the mean stage of water, the plane of reference. The dotted surlines beyond low water mark represent the bottom within the respective depths of 6 and 9 feet.

The characteristic soundings only are given on the map. They are selected from the numerous soundings taken in the survey so as to represent the figure of the bottom.

The Triangulation was executed in	1846 & '47.
The Topography	in	1847.
The Hydrography	in	1847.

The depth of water at a given point depends upon the greater or less supply by the rivers and upon the direction, force and duration of the wind. The Soundings are reduced to the mean depth found during 364 days in 1847-8, when observations were made at midnight, and from 4 A.M. to 8 P.M. hourly. At the entrance of the Pasquotank Southerly winds increase the depth of water and Northerly winds diminish it. On the average the depths vary however, but 2½ inches with Southerly and Northerly winds.

The greatest height during the series of observations was with the wind South'd. and Westw'd, and exceeded the least height, which was with the wind Northw'd. and Eastw'd. by 2 ft. 3½ inches.

Latitude of Elizabeth City Court H.	36° 18′ 04″
Longitude of do. do. West from }	76° 13′ 24″
Greenwich Observatory in time	5° 04′ 53″·6
Variation of the Magnetic Needle at Stevensons Pt. at the mouth of Perquimons R. as observed by C.O. Boutelle Asst. in Feb. 1847. }	1°·46′ West.

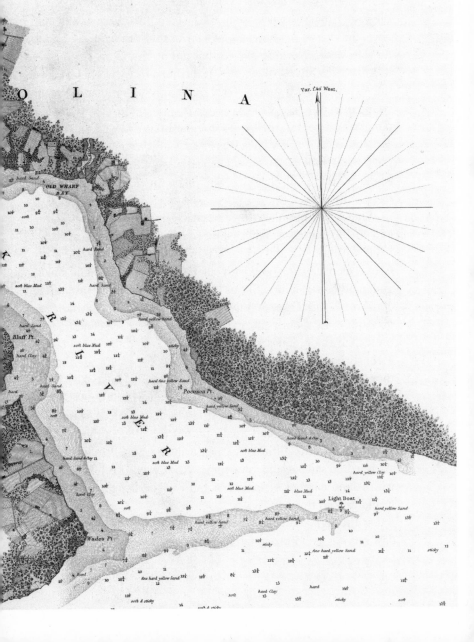

his cracked bare feet in mud where hogs had slept and heated it. He took food to his exiled mother in her little cabin out in the wet untillable woods where she had been sent to live once she became too old and infirm to work, and where he waited with her the time the patrollers were out searching all over for his older brother, the one who ran away and disappeared.

As Enoch Sawyer's ferryman on the dark Pasquotank River, the young slave was as close to the heart of this place as any man alive, for everything hereabouts—farms and timber, too—had to do with water. Nothing moved that did not move over and upon it. Elizabeth City, the new town at the horseshoe riverbend called the Narrows, just below the ferry route, was not even as old as the young man. Whenever Sawyer bade him leave the ferry-flat at the far side and go into the town for something, the youth could see for himself that this village was already all about ships and shipping. In its three yards, slaves such as he were the builders and the caulkers and the blacksmiths who made the new ships and overhauled the old.

What wharf there was in this small, busy place crowded often, and quickly, with oceangoing ships soon bound for the West Indies laden with juniper and cypress shingles brought down out of the Great Dismal Swamp and with oak barrel staves and metal spikes and handles and hoops. Slaves loaded the boats. Outbound, these craft would sail eighteen miles down the now-broad, baylike Pasquotank to its mouth and then cross the Albemarle Sound, continue many more miles where big hollow-backed waves built dangerously before the wind and raced miles over open water before they broke, and then head south, skirting around Roanoke Island, down the Pamlico to Shell Castle Island, Governor John Wallace's port of entry, with its warehouses and cribbed wharves just behind Ocracoke Inlet, and finally on out the inlet to the Atlantic Ocean and south-southeast to the Caribbean Sea. Presently these ships would sail back up, returning to the Carolina tidelands filled with island cargoes of molasses and rum and sugar, and slaves would unload them.

On the ferry-flat, the young black man went to school every day, serving as both seaman and captain, holding close what he heard and studying unceasingly what the white and black men did and said (and what they did not), and there was no shortage to what a country boy in such maritime employment could learn.

He heard talk of Tom Copper, the slave rebel leader with his army in the swamps, and of the men arrested and brought to court in Camden for plotting rebellion with Copper. That was back in 1802, and he remembered how the great fear of a slave uprising spread from his native Camden all across the Carolina northeast counties: Currituck, Hertford, Halifax, and Pasquotank. He remembered the slave Mingo who betrayed his own kind and turned in the supposed instigators, six black men hauled into court in Camden on what came to light as Mingo's untrue word alone and then, to the shock of all, found not guilty. And Mingo, having borne false witness, had his ears sliced away from his skull, though the officers of the court let him keep his lying lips.

And the young ferryman heard more talk of the big Dismal Swamp Canal just to the north of Elizabeth City and Camden, the twenty-two-mile muddy ditch that had been dug out and cut at for over a dozen years now by slaves with picks and shovels and saws, all gnawing punily at the Great Dismal Swamp and aiming to connect his river and his sound, the Albemarle, with the Elizabeth River and Chesapeake Bay. Already flatboats piled high with cedar and cypress shingles floated the shallow canal, and soon, he heard men say, trade would move between Elizabeth City and Norfolk on canalboats and shallow-draft sailing scows.

One dawn on Mister Enoch Sawyer's ferry-flat, Camden County men as black as the young ferryman told him what had occurred one night at the alehouse not too far downstream. They told him what they had seen and heard, as if it had happened the night before and not five years earlier.

A Hatterasman and his young son had sailed their bugeye straight up the Pasquotank against a fierce, cold north wind, coming up from the Outer Banks with bales of dried yaupon tarped on deck against the wind and spray. They had tied their boat off stem and stern at the Elizabeth City wharf, just a few logs stove down into the blueblack mud and sand—better some dock than none in all this wet and water-loving land. Without a word the Hatterasman strode to the alehouse door, his exhausted son, whipped from fighting wind and weather all that way, trudging behind, and for a moment the two of them stood in the grim light, silhouetted and still like statuary.

"Scarborough!" a man from deep inside cried out at the Hatterasman, and all those there—fishermen, sawyers, shingle-getters down from the Dismal Swamp—turned and gazed upon him. They knew at once from the name and the sound of the name that he was a Banker, an islander, and knew further what his cargo was, the holly that grew everywhere out on those long wide sandbars and that everyone there cured and brewed, as the Indians had shown them how to do, into a sedative, a purgative. It was the one and only thing the Bankers had way out there that they could bring to town and sell. From nearer to the door, a drunk laughed caustically and let loose his derisive cry.

"Kinnakeeters," he yelled. "Yaupon eaters!"

Before the barroom laughter died down, Scarborough stepped toward the man and, with one slamming right punch, knocked him cold. Then he stalked back with the boy across the mud lane to their boat and spent the cold night laid up with their bitter cargo.

The Camden County Negroes had seen it all from right there in the dockside street, though they feigned they had not, wanting no involvement in the slightest even by acknowledging themselves as witnesses, but now, on this cold early morning with enough years gone by, they could tell the young black ferryman, who took it all in, and thought it all through: *They do this even to their own kind. Drive their own away just like they drove my own brother away, just because he couldn't round up some cattle one night. So they sent him back out again and again till he couldn't stand it anymore, and what'd he do but go off and lie down in the woods underneath some leaves and freeze and die, and lie there unburied until buzzards came and ate out his eyes. . . .*

Sunup would come soon, plating the dark river with a golden light, and the three would wait for it and for a paying white man and horse, or wagon, to come along presently, and then the boy would set loose the ferry and work the pole and the sweep, the huge sculling-oar, and together they would cross the river back to Enoch Sawyer's on the Camden side.

They were all three of them slaves, and the young man's name was Moses Grandy.

After leaving Enoch Sawyer's employ the next year, Moses Grandy worked for George Furley, driving a two-wheel shingle cart back in the Great Dismal Swamp and hauling stacks and stacks of shingles from wherever they were riven back to a camp of lean-tos from which they were loaded onto shingle lighters and floated out of the swamp. The difference between a ferry-flat and a shingle flat, Moses Grandy regarded, was slight, and this plain and simple fact would soon serve him well, for he knew that a man who can run the one could run the other, if he were but allowed to do so.

Who would let him try his hand at other craft, and on other waters?

The year after that swamping, John Micheau hired Moses for fieldwork at his plantation in Camden County near Areneuse Creek. Micheau—a one-time dry-and-wet goods merchant in Elizabeth City who, in 1795, sold out to the merchant and ship-yard operator Charles Grice—was now a planter and brother-in-law to Moses's owner, James Grandy. Moses felt ill used here. He had become a waterman, for God's sake, not a fieldworker. Not a manservant, either—Micheau once kept him out day and night for a five-day bender in a Camden gambling house, Moses being there just to watch out for Micheau should anyone try and get the better of him, though Moses spent much of his guardian time dead tired and asleep on his feet. Micheau got two years' work out of him, till Richard Furley took Grandy on, allowing him to go out and labor for himself and share his earnings with this Furley, which pursuit continued for several years. Then owner James Grandy retrieved all the slaves he had inherited and leased out, continuing the Furley plan, only doubling the amount of earnings Moses had to return to James Grandy in order to keep laboring on his own account.

Through it all, wherever he was, Moses Grandy watched all the men who came and went on, those who met with Enoch Sawyer and James Grandy and at other times other men for whom he worked, on porches in town and country, on Water Street in Elizabeth City, along the road through the country from Elizabeth City to the river bridge that ran off through the swamp country to Moyock and north to Norfolk, at the edges of fields. Wherever white men of any worth at all met or gathered to talk and trade, he watched them, how they greeted and spoke and cajoled, how they did with each other in speech and manner, because he needed to find and know the one among all of them who would help him the most. He was young yet and had seen a rough go of things already, but he was old enough to know that his life should not be all brutish work and near starvation and standing on the ceremony and bad habits of white men. Tall and strong, he could work as hard as any of them, white or black, and could outwork most of them, this he knew. And that must count for something, maybe enough, for he knew, too, that his hard work was always noticed, his coming early and staying late, too, no matter what the task. And while he watched and worked he heard other black men cuss the whites, heard of would-be rebels and always of runaways, yet he kept his counsel and studied: he would not be shot or caught and dragged back to somewhere worse than he had already been, that was not for him. What he would do was learn and figure and cipher through it all how this world worked and make it work for him. He could do that, he was sure. And so he watched them all, knowing he would someday somehow settle on one man.

And Charles Grice, late of Philadelphia, now of Elizabeth City, turned out to be that one.

A merchant and shipyard owner, Grice also served as a trustee of the Elizabeth City Academy and as a commissioner to build Pasquotank County's courthouse, her prison, pillory, and stocks. Of real note and import to the slave, he was the husband of the sister of James Grandy, Moses Grandy's owner.

Legend had it—this from his daughter—that Grice had come into this country many years before, way back in 1785, sailed in through Ocracoke Inlet and gotten together with Enoch Sawyer and his brother Lemuel and made a bold but not bold enough attempt to buy from some farm crone the land for a new town. But the old woman refused them, and Grice went on back to Philadelphia for a spell, finally coming back a second time and with more money and offering it this time to tavern-keeper Betsy Tooley, throwing in the added inducements of a silk and calico dress—or two dresses, one of silk and one of calico, it depended on who was telling the story—and the promise to name the town for her. Yet in truth, Grice did not lay out the town and doubtful had anything to do with its naming. But he was here early on, Moses knew this for certain, and had been here ever since Moses was old enough to remember men and men's names, and he knew Mister Grice to be one of the main men in the new town.

———

Grice—once a private in Philadelphia's Third Company, State Fencibles, back in the Revolution—took charge of defending Elizabeth City against the British, and he set to building two "Jackson batteries of tobacco w/ bags of sand, for want of cotton" (as he would write to James Iredell much later, in 1829) on the river down at Cobb Point, between Forbes Bay and Davis Bay, and Moses Grandy wished he could be requisitioned to go and help him. When the British blockaded Chesapeake Bay and closed Hampton Roads to the sea on the day after Christmas 1812, suddenly there was only one riverine way for goods to go into and out of Norfolk on the south side: the Elizabeth River's south branch, the Dismal Swamp Canal, and the Pasquotank running down to the Albemarle Sound.

The merchant, the man who moved and warehoused and sold goods of all sorts, saw at once that the new war with the British and their Hampton Roads blockade was throwing things his way. Charles Grice sought out his brother-in-law James Grandy in Camden and made a deal and shook hands with him, then found the lanky twenty-one-year-old black man he had been watching and making note of for years and shook Moses Grandy's hand, too, and in the cold, spare winter shadows of the bare cypress along the blackriver shore Grice said: "Moses, you've run that ferry and been a field hand long enough, and I want you to work for me: you're a freightboat captain now."

The Wharf on the Pasquotank River

Elizabeth City, North Carolina

Boatman dance, boatman sing
Boatman do most anything
When the boatman gets on shore
Spends his money and works for more.

Moses Grandy was used to going to bed cold and hungry in a cabin in Camden and then waking up no less cold, no less hungry, a hoecake scarcely enough to stave it off, turning out at first light, the ground frozen, he underclad and unshod, and the only way to warm his feet was to rouse a hog and stand in the absolute mud where the hog had lain all night and let that rare warm earth wake his flesh and move his own blood. Now he was Charles Grice's boatman, and Mister Grice saw to it that the man he had to trust with no small part of his commercial life the fifty miles up to Norfolk and then back again did not go to work on the water hungry or cold or barefoot. The young man got a griddle cake, a salted herring, an old blanket refashioned into a coat with a rope belt to hold it closed, an old pair of boots, and a big cypress boat.

Grice put Grandy in command of a rude sailing barge, two huge dug-out cypress logs with a long plank keel joining them, here in North Carolina called a periauger, most of forty feet long overall and low with room aplenty for barrels of flour, barrels of fish, and decking enough that a hog or a goat or small cow could be happy just long enough to reach the market up the way. His was a heavy craft, with a pair of sails and a small cabin forward, yet without a name, and it could be pulled, poled, rowed, scull-oared, sailed, whatever motive force was necessary and available. Sometimes there might be a second such boat, sometimes two more. However many there were, Moses Grandy commanded them all.

Wintertime, wartime, he cared not—in a life and in a world of captivity he was at last master of something important: his own movements for many days at a time. Cold, what was that? Start early, start while it was still dark and the hard winter cold had its rough grip upon all these broad low tidelands, when the moon hung in the night clouds and the black river seemed frozen to its edges. This was still a cold he could live with somehow. Raise those two heavy Bermuda sails and catch the bare breath of wind and move slowly away to the north, in this cypress freightboat past the cypress sentinels lining the river's edge, some faintly lit by the setting moon, some silhouetted, and Grandy and his crew, guarded by the very trees, moved upriver like free men.

In the clear, frigid morning, the sun poured a bright light without warmth over the black water. A tall blue heron stalked the shallows of the side woods as Grandy's freightboat crawled northward toward Norfolk, the heron croaking hoarsely at him as he passed slowly and she took flight, following the serpentine Pasquotank upriver, the Moccasin Track scarcely navigable for a working craft but a free and easy range for a big silvergray-and-blue bird on the hunt.

As the morning advanced, a redtail hawk flew, planing the sky high above Moses Grandy, whose day was a hunt of his own.

Mister Grice's goods got to get to Norfolk.
War or no war, I guide these boats.
I guide these boats.

———

I guide these boats up and down the old canal
Up and down the old canal, night and day
That's my way.

Moses Grandy worked at this for months, for years, till he became Captain Grandy, widely known and addressed as such.

What a momentous thing it was to move freely in the world, to study wind and wave and make predictions and direct actions rather than bear the brunt of someone else's, Grandy mused unceasingly. The length and breadth of the journeying to and from Norfolk, the power of the trust placed in him by Mister Grice in Elizabeth City and, on the upper end, by Mister Moses Myers, the merchant in Norfolk—these at moments seemed as liberating as liberation itself. With Grice his de facto employer, Captain Grandy now worked on shares, his pay directly related to the freight he safely brought down the waterways from Myers's wharf on the river in Norfolk to Grice's warehouse and shop in Elizabeth City.

Approaching the Norfolk wharves for the freight-gathering upper end of these trips, Grandy could always spy Myers with ease—long, lean-faced Myers with the short gray hair and the dark bushy eyebrows. Myers and his wife, Eliza, had been in Norfolk twenty-five years and were its first Jews, people said, and theirs was among the first brick homes laid up after the Revolution, a big one, a showplace with gilding on the living-room mantel, and with an octagon wing added on by none other than Benjamin Latrobe, the great architect who would also build the U.S. Capitol and the Washington Canal and much more. Moses Grandy heard—not from Myers himself but from other men around Hampton Roads, and not all at once—how Myers dealt with the French, ran the Bank of Richmond, and ran the council of Norfolk.

Good to have such friends, thought Grandy, men who trust you like the sun.

One Thursday morning Moses Grandy left his wife of eight months at Enoch Sawyer's plantation and came with Grice's freightboats from Elizabeth City on up the Pasquotank, where the reaches and bends became so short and convoluted. By Friday he had locked through at South Mills and continued north on the Dismal Swamp Canal. He and his men on the boats poled and bushwhacked, put men ashore with ropes, and even put up a little sail if there were so much as a breath of breeze from east or south. West winds did them little good, for the curtain of green on the canal's west bank cut them off. Captain Grandy poled from the starboard bow of the lead boat—the other men would work no harder than he, after all, and no harder than they could see him poling. Presently from up on the canalbank road came the clatter of wagon wheels and the dull jangle of trace chains, and Moses Grandy turned and saw a gang of slaves, some trudging on foot, some on the wagon, coming ahead on and catching up with his boats, northbound to Norfolk for sale, just like the lumber in his boats.

Moses Myers, merchant of Norfolk, Virginia

A woman cried out from the gang on the road: "Moses, my dear!"

Grandy's grip on the pole loosened and he let it go, and the pole scraped noisily along the gunwhale and then fell into the dark water, as he stood in shock at the recognition that the woman who had called out to him from the group of Negroes on the wagon was his wife, who then said only: "I am gone."

"Whoa!" Captain Grandy called to his men. He grabbed another pole and ran to port and pushed and found purchase somehow in the muddy water. Snubbing the starboard bow into the canalbank, he grabbed a line, leapt off, tied the line around a gumstump, and climbed up the bank.

"For God's sake, Mister Rogerson," he shouted to the man on horseback with a brace of pistols. "Have you bought my wife?"

"Yes."

"Why? What has she done?" Grandy approached the other.

"Nothing," said Rogerson, drawing a pistol. "Enoch Sawyer wanted money. You go near that wagon where she's at, I'll shoot you."

"May I shake her hand?" asked Captain Grandy in anguish.

"No. You stand over there on the side of the road—don't you get near her—and you can talk to her."

What could he say, though? He was one of the strongest men in this part of the world, but he was wholly undone by this unexpected moment. What on earth could he say, or do? He was beside himself, rebuking himself, thinking, *I am as weak as water.*

"Mister Rogerson, may I give her a dram?"

"Burgess," said Rogerson from his horse to another mounted man. "Get down and carry it to her." His pistol was still drawn.

Captain Grandy pulled a few silver bits from his pocket and handed them to Burgess for his wife. His gaze followed the man's paces, the handing over of the silver, the despair in his woman's empty eyes as she received it. He could not, he dared not, look anywhere else but at her, nor she but at him—for the both of them knew this was it, their last moment anywhere near each other forever. Grandy listened to Burgess's footfalls as he strode back to his horse and remounted.

"Let's go!" Rogerson called out loudly, and his order echoed off the deep-woods wall across the canal. The two horses, and the wagon before them and the men on foot before it, all began again.

"Farewell!" Moses Grandy cried out to her as the doomed troupe moved northward, and he knew he loved her as he loved his own life, and he feared—knew—that he would never see her again in this world.

Rogerson reined his horse with his left hand and kept his right, holding the pistol, aloft so Grandy could see it well. Once he was thirty yards up the road, he turned and looked back at Grandy, who had not moved at all, and then he, with show, holstered the gun and turned forward and did not regard Moses Grandy again.

Captain Grandy walked out into the road and stared after his wife and all the rest as they drifted away up the long straight canalbank trace toward its vanishing point, till after a few minutes he could no longer tell whether they were still moving, or if they were just some sculpted misery in the long lane ahead of him.

He would never know how long he stood there. Finally he staggered back down the bank and his men reached out and helped him onto the lead boat. His face was as wet as the pole they handed him, which they had fished out of the water. Moving to the bow again and drawing himself up—with what strength from what well, who knew?—Captain Grandy at last dropped the pole at an angle to the bank and, casting off, said loudly, so the men on the other boats behind the lead craft could hear him, too: "We need to be in Deep Creek before dark."

I guide these boats up and down the old canal
Up and down the old canal, night and day
That's my way.

Elizabeth City, North Carolina

CIRCA 1817

For two years and more, Captain Grandy had been paying James Grandy, his childhood playmate and, now, his owner, bit by bit small sums against the six-hundred-dollar fee the white man had said he would take for Grandy's freedom. For each payment handed over, the freightboat captain had exacted a receipt, and he had kept his receipts on his person and guarded them with his life. This was Mister Grice's very good idea, and Grice had backed Moses Grandy all the way in this great effort.

Court week came to Camden, and the time was nigh. With one final payment, the fee was to be satisfied, and James Grandy would now stride into the courthouse and file with the Camden County clerk of court the free papers for Captain Moses Grandy. All James Grandy asked of the captain was that he give his owner all those receipts from all those payments over all those many months.

The two men were standing at the crossroads, within sight of the courthouse, and Captain Grandy did as he was asked.

What James Grandy did with Captain Grandy's receipts, though, was to take them in his hands and tear them with his thumbs and forefingers into irrecoverable shreds, letting them drop to the dirt and drift in the breeze, as if they were nothing more than breadcrumbs for sparrows and mourning doves.

"Why are you doing this?" Captain Grandy cried out in alarm.

"It doesn't matter," his owner replied. "I will get you your free papers when the court is in session."

And then James Grandy walked off, not to the courthouse but to a rude hut down the way where another white man kept a billiard table and clay jugs full of corn whiskey. Court week was always good for billiards and drinks all around.

Moses Grandy waited. He waited believing that the God of laws and man could not allow anything to occur other than the true way to his freedom. He waited as court week in Camden came and went. Yet by its end the only door James Grandy had darkened was that of the tavern.

Over the river in Elizabeth City, Captain Grandy now went to work aboard a lumber schooner. He went out touring the Albemarle Sound, filling the schooners with juniper planks or cypress planks or pine, whatever had been milled and dried and was stacked up drying along the creeks and rivers awaiting shipment.

From the Narrows and down the broad Pasquotank River, the

Shore of Albemarle Sound

lumber schooner sailed, with Moses Grandy aboard her. The ship would now traverse the forty-mile length of Albemarle Sound, south side and north, and load up, collecting planks from isolated farms along the creeks and rivers that fed the sound, for lumber was what flowed out to the West Indies in trade.

In the little mills in the backwaters, some of the saws cut planks by up and down motion, as men kept pressure on the log and the carriage upon which they bore it against the blade. With more power, though, like the power the six-foot drop, or head, from the outflow canal off the north side of Lake Phelps afforded Josiah Collins of Somerset, a circular sawblade could be run. The cypress and the cedar cut easily, and, whether sliced by saws into planks or riven into big shingles, the world wanted it, and pine planks, too, and there was pine aplenty in the lowlands.

So first across the sound, before the wind lightly from the northeast, and into Bull's Bay and down toward Colonial Beach, to which the lighters from Somerset had come down the dark

Scuppernong River with their lumber. Then west to Mackeys Creek and into that black water, then on farther west and into the mouth of the Roanoke River and up the brown water to Plymouth and more lumber—how it slid and lay belowdecks and Lord, you could get a lot of roughhewn planks to fit and get out of that place. Now on back to the sound and into Swan Bay, up the Cashie, and over the Albemarle to Edenton Bay and that old port and its wrought-iron, big house balconies for more, then up the Yeopim River, staying well clear of Batts Grave, the island at that river's mouth and its shoals, for more still, and the Perquimans River and the Little River, too. You didn't take a half a load down to the islands, or three-quarters, not as much as they were cutting, as fast as the woods were coming down around here now—you took a loaded boat, Moses Grandy knew, and you did not lose a stick.

———

After the lumber schoonering, Moses Grandy again captained freightboats up to Norfolk, and upon his arrival at Moses Myers's store there, Myers appeared at the door with another shipper, a man named Trewitt who inquired of Grandy: "Who chartered your boats?"

"Mister Sutton, in Elizabeth City," Captain Grandy said. "For Mister Grice's store."

"And to whom do you belong?"

"Well," said Grandy, "I used to belong to Mister James Grandy, but I have bought myself."

Trewitt seemed not to have heard Grandy, for he glided over Grandy's reply. "I will buy you."

"What are you talking about, Trewitt?" said Moses Myers. "You can't buy a man who has already bought himself."

"We'll see about that," Trewitt replied. "I'll buy him as soon as I reach Elizabeth City."

Captain Grandy was used to hearing white men talk, brag, conjecture, and propose things they might or might not ultimately do or deliver, yet he had not known this man Trewitt well. He had no way of knowing why he was speaking with such smug certitude, or what it might mean. A couple of days later, after sailing south and delivering the cargo to Mister Grice, Grandy and Grice walked together to the customhouse, there to meet up with Trewitt.

"Well, Captain," Trewitt announced briskly to Grandy when he saw him. "I have bought you."

Mister Grice said coldly: "Let us have no nonsense; go and settle with him."

"I have bought him, by God," Trewitt continued.

"No, you haven't. You can't," said Grice.

In a furious knot the three men then walked to Grice's home, and no sooner did Trewitt settle up with Moses Grandy over the freight Grandy had brought down from Norfolk than he leapt to his feet proclaiming: "Now I will show you, Mister Grice, whether I am a liar or not." Trewitt pulled a paper from out of his coat and shoved it before Grice, who read it swiftly and darkened before calling his wife. When she came quickly into the room and read the paper and then burst into tears, Grandy was suddenly undone, and he wept as well.

The paper Trewitt had presented them with was a bill of sale from James Grandy to Trewitt, transferring the ownership of Moses Grandy to Trewitt for six hundred dollars.

Astonished and infuriated, Moses Grandy and the two Grices flew from Trewitt and sought out James Grandy. At Woods's boardinghouse, they found him playing billiards and there they bearded him over his treachery. Captain Grandy asked him bluntly: "Master James, have you sold me?" When James Grandy said no, Moses Grandy said bitterly, "Yes, you have!"

The man at billiards was caught and he knew it. James Grandy dropped his cue stick and stumbled and staggered from room to room crying and groaning, though there was no remorse in it, only his chagrin in being challenged and found out and called out before others.

"Why?" his sister, Mrs. Grice, asked him unceasingly. "Why, why?"

"They laughed at me," James Grandy sobbed. "Everyone laughed at me. Said I was stupid, too stupid, and that I'd been outsmarted and skinned by a nigger."

"Nobody's skinned you!" Charles Grice thundered at him. "You made a clear deal with Moses Grandy and he's paid you and you've done him wrong. You're nothing but a thief! God damn your eyes, James Grandy!"

"Done nothing wrong!" said the other. "Moses Grandy was mine all along, and everything he done and said and made and paid, it was never his, it was mine all along. And he's got nothing to show for it noways."

Then in disgust and anger the boardinghouse mistress and the tenants and the Grices all forced James Grandy to the front door and out through it. Suddenly he was in the dirt street standing alone, except for his sailcloth bag tossed out after him, and in his fierce invincible ignorance he alone knew just how right he was. As soon as she could file papers, Mrs. Grice would sue her own brother over Moses Grandy's cause, but in the end the court would hold with James Grandy. The court would hold that all of Moses's doings, all his work and money and two years to make it, always were the property of James Grandy and that no one else but he had ever had any standing regarding the fate of Moses Grandy, slave in Camden County.

Until the moment that Mister Trewitt became his new owner.

Before the law, and in the affairs of Trewitt and James Grandy, it was as if Captain Grandy had never paid James Grandy the first two bits, let alone a full six hundred dollars, toward his freedom.

The day this judgment landed, Moses Grandy came away from Camden, taking the same ferry he had so often run, but now as a traveler, walked on from Knobbs Creek into town, and returned to the Water Street wharf and to a freightboat there soon to be bound for Norfolk. He took in his lines, shoved off, and was away. He put up some canvas, set men fore and aft with poles, laid his hand upon the tiller.

Someone at the courthouse said it would be a cold day in hell before Grandy ever walked free in North Carolina, but, grim as he felt, he knew better. The freightboat tacked slowly up the broad reach above Elizabeth City, between the mainland and the north side of Goat Island.

Captain Grandy worked on.

Enoch Sawyer's Home on the Pasquotank River

Camden County, North Carolina

JUNE 10, 1818

Make ready. Make ready. Make nice. Polish silver and count spoons and recount spoons and let none be missing. Fluff pillows that will not be slept on. Beat rugs that will not be walked upon or even seen, and then beat rugs that will soon be trod upon by the President of the United States, Mister James Monroe. These were the watchwords at the home of Enoch Sawyer hard by the Pasquotank River—this was what the new, second wife of Moses Grandy heard, and nearly all she heard: *Make ready. Make nice.*

Mister Monroe had sailed down the Potomac and the Chesapeake Bay to Norfolk upon the steamboat *Roanoke*, landing at Newton's Wharf, Norfolk, after a trip of only twenty-seven hours. He had stayed at Major Farange's ordinary on the Dismal Swamp Canal, even gone up and seen Lake Drummond in the middle of the swamp, coming down from which one of his entourage, Commodore Elliott, was thrown from the Navy yawl when it struck a stump and was pitched into the dark water and muddy peat. The President was now coming to Sawyer's Ferry and to Mister Enoch Sawyer's fine house to be entertained before going on back to Norfolk and a big public dinner at the Exchange Coffee House. For Enoch Sawyer was his ally, his appointee and the brother of another ally, Congressman Lemuel Sawyer, sickly yet a Monroe enthusiast, a dependable vote.

When the President was in the Dismal, when he stood beside the Pasquotank, he heard the choiring of a million warblers come back this spring from the tropics and nesting everywhere, bright yellow prothonotaries shuttle-cocking vividly about, the shy drab Swainson's flitting surreptitiously, hiding out in the switchcane. He smelled the lemony yellow jessamine in bloom, vining all over the swamp forests all around him, and the grapevines intertwined with honeysuckle, the air redolent with its sweet Southern scent, and cow lilies, too, their small yellow orbs for flowers. Now and again a great blue heron glided by, and always, somewhere in the middle distance, turkey buzzards soared, black vultures flapping and gliding, over the deep entangling jungle.

In Elizabeth City before the dinner party at Enoch Sawyer's, the President and his entourage had been feted and served green turtle at the new City Hotel (where all heard Commodore Elliot cursing inside his carriage at his bemuddied self and at the President who planned such excursions, till the President himself leaned into the carriage and said wryly, "What is the matter, friend Elliott?"). And then it was Sawyer's place on the Pasquotank that would for a few hours be the center of the American world, as here came President Monroe and his troupe. For the wife of Moses Grandy, this Mister Monroe could be a king as easily as a president, either being so distant; he could be anybody, or nobody at all. The words she heard were not coming to her from kings or presidents, though; they came down from the people who ran and owned this place, whose name was on the waters, Sawyer's Creek, from the man and the wife of the man who owned her, Enoch Sawyer, Esquire, and Mrs. Sawyer: *Make ready, Grandy. Polish the silver. Count the spoons. Count them again. And make nice.*

Dismal Swamp Canal and Lake Drummond Hotel

Newbegun Creek

Southern Pasquotank County, North Carolina

For two and a half years now, Moses Grandy had captained Mister Trewitt's pair of canalboats between Elizabeth City and Norfolk, and now it was the night before Christmas and Moses had just settled up with Trewitt at his waterside office in Elizabeth City for this most recent trip. Grandy had at last paid the man off, a second six hundred dollars gone to this second owner, a second bid for his freedom, and all he wanted to do right now was head back upriver to Enoch Sawyer's plantation in Camden and spend Christmas in the arms of his wife, God bless her.

This is what he had slaved for.

Yet Trewitt had something different in mind for Captain Grandy this evening. Trewitt needed to send him in the opposite direction, down the Pasquotank River to Newbegun Creek to deliver a letter to Mister William Muse there. The task was worth two dollars to Moses Grandy if he would just do this one last thing for Mister Trewitt.

Another merchant, a man named John Shaw, overheard the two men talking and walked into Trewitt's office. Shaw had a schooner laden and at anchor here at the Narrows, bound for Newbegun Creek for Mister Ambrose Knox there, and no one as yet to captain it downriver. Shaw offered five dollars to Captain Grandy to make the transit.

I guide these boats. . . .

Seven dollars Moses Grandy would then have, between Trewitt's and Shaw's money, to bring to his wife on Christmas Day, and she now carrying their child. So he took to the river, set sail on Shaw's craft, and made his way eight miles downstream. When he reached Newbegun Creek, most of a mile wide at its mouth, he lowered his sails and dropped anchor in the dark and waited for the waning Cold Moon to rise and light his way into the creek. Before long moonlight flooded the river, laid a ribbon on the water behind him and cast a stark white light over the broad Newbegun bay before him. I wish I had more coat, he thought. Seven dollars, he thought.

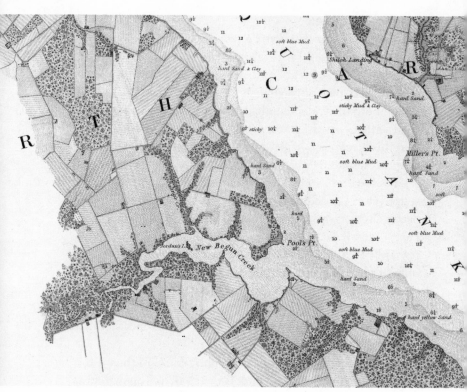

Newbegun Creek, on the west side of the Pasquotank River

Captain Grandy raised his sails and got under way again. Coming into Newbegun Creek from the river, he crossed a broad reach of nearly two miles, passing Palin's Creek to the north—that was old Broomfield, where they said the county's first courthouse once was. Now he must ease around along the north side of the creek to clear Jordan's Island, a squiggle of low land just a few hundred feet long set nearly in the middle of the stream, before the Newbegun meanders began. The wharf he sought lay at the bottom of the third horseshoe bend, and moonlight led him right on into it.

At the Newbegun wharf he docked at last, tied the schooner up fore and aft, and unloaded his cargo beneath the moon. Then the captain and his men slept heavy against the cold in the small ship's rude cabin, wrapped in old stiff blankets on the cabin floor. In the morning Grandy got the goods safely conveyed to Ambrose Knox, and then he went on to his second task, delivering Mister Trewitt's letter to William Templeman Muse, master of the great plantation Westmoreland and Pasquotank County's clerk of court as well.

A thin sheet of ice lay across the black water this morning. No breeze stirred the Spanish moss in the cypress and gum trees. The Newbegun swamp was cold and still, and walking up the plank path through the cypress, naked except for their clusters of seed pods, the cypress knees all about, Moses Grandy's footfalls startled a deer, spooked it from under a fallen oak where it had slept, and the deer's exploding out from its bed in turn startled Moses and gave him a shake. Canada geese were flying and honking overhead, and the *chit-chit* of winter birds sounded through the woods. From a huge dead and debarked pine a pileated woodpecker started at the man's approach and flew straight through the swamp thicket not ten feet in front of him. The Lord-God bird! Grandy came up out of the swamp and onto the Newbegun road, entered the plantation lane a hundred yards to the east— *Morning sun'll be good after that cold boat, these iced-up woods*— and began a long, slow, half-a-mile walk south toward the farm's big house.

This was Westmoreland, the former Virginian William Muse's Pasquotank plantation paradise, getting torn out of this jungle bit by bit, a twelve-room house with verandas in the midst of a thousand acres and smokehouses and barns and a blacksmith's and pear and peach, cherry and apple and plum trees where before only blue-iris flags and bluebell and yellow jessamine grew wild. Moses Grandy was striding up the narrow road, first in the long shade cast by the swamp woods, then with the rising eastern sun at his side, toward the heart of the plantation, where a scuppernong vine covered half an acre of ground, and where in spring and summer the young white women sang:

Dogwood blossom on a cypress tree
If you want to kiss a pretty girl, come kiss me

No dogwood this cold Christmas morning, he thought, and no one for me to kiss, not yet, till back up the river to my wife in Camden. But this would not take long, he thought. Mister Muse may ask Moses Grandy to wait long enough for Muse to draft a letter in reply. Or maybe not. The captain could be back at the Newbegun wharf casting off lines in an hour—with a fair breeze he might make it upriver to town by early afternoon, get to his wife in Camden before dark. He might see her in the last of the Christmas daylight after all. He was still stiff from sleeping in that cold cabin shipboard, but the warmth of the sun felt good and stretching his legs did, too, as he drew closer and closer to the house at the head of the lane, at last reaching it and climbing a half a dozen broad stairs and now standing upon the veranda, holding his hat in one hand, the letter in the other, and knocking on the big unpainted front door.

Presently he heard an iron latch slide within and the door swung slowly open and sunlight flooded the dark front hall. William Muse stood before him and beckoned him inside the hall and took the envelope from him and opened it and withdrew the paper.

"Well," Muse said, after slowly reading the letter, and then a second time, "well."

"Yes, sir," said Moses Grandy. "You needing me to wait?"

"Moses, do you know what this letter says?"

"No, sir. Mister Trewitt just asked me to bring it to you. And it's sealed, and even if it wasn't, I can't read, and I wouldn't look at it no how."

"Yes, I know that. Everyone trusts you. What it says is you now belong to me."

"Belong! How?" asked Captain Grandy, shocked, his hand falling against a stair rail to steady himself. "What way?"

"Don't you recollect when Trewitt chartered Wilson Sawyer's brig to the West Indies?"

"Of course I do."

At that same time, Muse told Grandy, Trewitt borrowed six hundred dollars from him, given by Muse only after Trewitt signed a mortgage, with Moses Grandy the collateral for the note. Yet Muse had thought all along, he allowed, that Trewitt would fulfill his obligation and pay off this note. "I should not have taken a mortgage on you," Muse said to him. "I really thought Trewitt would take it up." But he had not and now his business had failed, and William Muse was out six hundred dollars of good money—he must now have hard cash or Grandy one, and there was no cash forthcoming from Trewitt.

I paid him. Paid him every cent I owed him. Over two years I paid him.

So Grandy it was.

A sudden, vertiginous fury and grief overcame the captain, a swoon of incredulity driving him back out into the Christmas daylight. What was seven dollars to take to his wife now, when he had lost another six hundred, along with his freedom because of an ill-begotten bargain between two other men, one of whom, Trewitt, had to have known—*Right while he was taking my last cash!*—that he and his business were doomed?

How could he live?

Moses Grandy flung himself out of Muse's home and ran crying, howling, stumbling across the stubble and, as he took to the thick woods, moaning among the cypress and pines and winter briars of the Newbegun morass over his own doom, he felt himself to be a crazed fool, cursed by God, wishing this wilderness swamp would open up and swallow him whole. Were he not delirious he would be dead in his tracks, ruined by another man's ruin.

However faithful he was and long had been, however devotedly he moved the boats up and down the waterways, he would never be free: he was cheated, defrauded, stopped short again. Nothing would ever change. A man may as well let the briars shred his rough clothes and then rip his shins and then walk into the two-mile river beyond the jungle and drown himself for once and all and be done with this world.

Yet he had a wife he loved.

The cold morning sun lit the farm, the cornstubble stitching in the fields, and the pineywoods all around. Moses Grandy staggered, stumbled, tripped into vinetangles, tried not to fall, wanted to fall, the weight on his chest a horror. Over his own cries, past the ragged choking he felt, and heard, in his throat, he heard too his footfalls in the sucking mud, and past that he dreamt he heard his name and knew he was worse than cursed by God—he was mocked by Him. Another wilderness, another Moses, yet no tablets, no guidance, no promise of anything this time except bondage upon bondage, endless into eternity and on beyond that. *Go on*, he cried out. *Go on! Burn me in that burning bush, make me like salt, smite me hip and thigh and flood the whole wretched world again—go on!* And every time he caught his ragged breath, he heard his name on the light icy wind and wanted God to find him here and be done with him.

But it was not God calling him—it was only William Muse's black manservant, standing at the edge of the Newbegun swamp and crying out to him over and over: "Moses! Moses Grandy, come back!" Captain Grandy wanted not to hear, feigned that he did not, until his fury settled coldly in his gut and his broken heart longed for his wife, and at last he did come back, limping now and his face bleeding, and he stumbled with the servant's help back up to the clerk of court's home, where inside from Muse, who now spoke slowly and formally to him, he learned his real fate.

Mister Enoch Sawyer, the customs collector in Camden, whose ferry Moses Grandy had run across the Pasquotank above the Narrows in years past, wanted to buy and own him, that was what else Trewitt let Muse know in the letter. Wanted Grandy to captain Sawyer's shingle and timber operations in the Great Dismal Swamp. Wanted Grandy to know that, should he refuse to submit, he might no longer approach or see his wife, still a slave at Sawyer's plantation on the river, and if he tried to, he risked being flogged or shot dead.

In no time, Moses Grandy would belong to Enoch Sawyer.

How could he go back to Enoch Sawyer's plantation and tell all this to his wife?

Regardless of what Captain Grandy had earned and was due— the mute cypress lining the waterways bearing witness on his behalf as he soon sailed bitterly back out the creek to the river—this was what he had gotten. Christmas had come to Newbegun Creek. Christmas had come to the Albemarle.

Christmas had come to Moses Grandy.

The Wind That Blows, 1820

Fevers are abroad in the new nation, one of them a sectionalism become so virulent and vehement the only way for the country to survive it is to drink from two jars, two opposing medicines, at the same time. The first prescription is Maine, admitted to the federal union as a free state on the Ides of March 1820, and the second is Missouri, admitted in exchange as a slave state a year later. Congress makes these acts less than five years after Francis Scott Key and George Washington's nephew Bushrod joined forces with the Reverend Robert Finley from New Jersey and created the American Colonization Society, a group intending to solve the Negro question by enabling black Americans to emigrate to an African homeland. The slavery-antislavery fever subsides, but it does not die; it merely remits.

Another heat, a fierce, abject frontier godliness, roars unslaked through the blood of many thousands of Americans, people who endure hardscrabble loneliness in small towns and farmsteads all winter long and then pack assembly halls and flood into encampments in fields where fiery country preachers, who have cut their oratorical eyeteeth making barn rafters ring, and shapenote singers, their voices edgier than axe blades, hold forth beneath brush-arbor shelters all across the backcountry.

President Monroe, whom General Andrew Jackson calls "Jim," warns the world in a few words to Congress, just prior to Christmas 1823, that the Western hemisphere is the American hemisphere and is off limits: no further European colonies need appear. It will take one whale of a navy for a country that does not yet even know the shape of its own coasts to patrol the Gulf of Mexico, the Caribbean islands, and the Latin American coasts and try and enforce Jim Monroe's tall order.

Maffitt, 1819–1834

50 North Latitude, 40 West Longitude

FEBRUARY 22, 1819

All three masts—fore, main, and mizzen—carried their sails unfurled from the yards as the square-rigged ship pounded away in the wintertime North Atlantic Ocean, bound from Ireland to New York. One of her passengers in steerage was Ann Carnic Maffitt, a gravid young woman whose time was nigh, traveling to join her husband, Reverend John Newland Maffitt, in Connecticut.

As she lay in her small berth belowdecks, attended by women, she cried out for him, moaned for him, howled at times as if to drown out the banshee wind that blew over the sea. No longer could she tell how large the ocean swells were, or how often they were coming, or if the ship were bucking fore and aft or twisting in opposite directions, or both—her body seemed to be twisting and swelling on its own, and in her near delirium she could no longer divide herself and her labors from those of the ship.

Are there storms on this ocean tonight? Ann Maffitt asked. *No storms like the one within me*, she answered. *Where is my husband, the preacher who has promised me heavens unceasing and a living world in motion forever and always?* The Good Lord knew, she had just now all the motion a body could want, or stand. Where was the man with whom she plighted her troth, who pledged his love and then saw his future not in Dublin or even in Ireland or England anywhere, but in New England on the ocean's far shore? Red skies at morning, red skies at night, warning, delight, and blow ye winds, heigh-ho, ten thousand miles away. . . .

When Ann Maffitt awakened she held heaven in her arms, a baby boy, healthy of limb, breathing easily in time with her own breathing, wanting to sleep yet also wanting to try out his fingers and his mouth upon her, hearing uncomprehending his first music, songs from *Moore's Melodies* from his mother's lips, flinching at the sharp hits of bootheels on the deckplanking above. And if it were a rolling sea beyond the mother and child, she scarcely knew it, for she now felt a great calm like that of a beautiful day dawning after a hurricane, and she heard faintly the sailors' exchanges on deck: "Steady as she goes, mate. Steady as she goes."

Three months of sailing under all this canvas and they would fetch up in America in the spring. The mother had in those first moments of his life named the baby boy for his absent father, yet she already sensed, well before the 21st of April, when Reverend Maffitt came down the post road to meet them in the harbor of the city of New York, that somehow her babe born at sea might in a deeper way be allegiant to another, to whom someday he would be duty bound.

John Newland Maffitt Jr. was a son of Neptune.

Cumberland County, North Carolina

1824

Ellerslie, a Sandhills farm, sat smartly in the longleaf pine country of Cumberland County outside of Fayetteville, North Carolina. The master of the estate was Doctor William Maffitt, happily married three years now to Margaret Adam. He served his community as a physician, dutiful, abhorring improvidence and poverty wherever he encountered it, especially ashamed of it in his own family, most particularly in his preacher brother, John Maffitt, away in the North. For years now he had been hearing of it, and he was scarcely surprised to receive a letter from Ann Maffitt that this brother—already a Methodist before he ever left Ireland—had become too moved by the Holy Spirit to minister only to one flock in one place. Called and compelled, Reverend Maffitt now intended to tour the whole of New England like an itinerant tinker and spread the Lord's Word wherever two or three would gather together in His name and listen—in chapels and public halls, to be sure, but also on street corners and village greens, public houses and taverns, if need be.

Praise God!

Reverend Maffitt meant to put himself on the Boston Post Road and on back roads from the salt ponds of southeastern Massachusetts to the Berkshire hills in the west and the Green Mountains along the ragged border between New Hampshire and Vermont. If they needed him atop Mount Washington, he would go up there too and howl louder than the tempest winds. Himself, alone, on the road—but not his family, which was collapsing. This was not what Ann Carnic Maffitt had been promised, and she had made up her mind to leave him, she wrote her brother-in-law. She had found a way through friends to go out west to Texas, where she would take her daughters and start anew and make a stand running a boardinghouse.

Her son, John, though, what of him?

Ann Maffitt could not manage them all.

She had a hope, and Doctor Maffitt answered it and spoke right up for young John—he wrote Ann in return that he would soon come north for the boy to bring him back, a five-year-old adoptee to live and be raised in North Carolina among his cousins, and a big down-home welcome to him.

Once ensconced at Ellerslie, the boy found at once that his uncle's country place suited him beyond anyone's expectations, and he ranged freely, energetically, all over the farm fields and woods and creeks, chunking rocks at the redheaded woodpeckers that deviled the cherry trees of Old Man McPherson, the neighbor, one keen thought burning daily in his heart and mind: *I love every blade of grass on the old place.*

Cumberland County, North Carolina

MARCH 4, 1825

An astoundingly heavy rain was general all over south central Carolina, falling upon the Sandhills and running off in rivulets beside and upon the roads and in gravel gullies edging the small farm fields, cascading torrentially through the longleaf pine barrens and the lonesome turpentine camps of the upper Cape Fear Valley. Doctor Maffitt left his horse saddled in the barn upon returning from his morning calls. A sheet of water stood in the yard between barn and house, and he splashed through it rapidly in crossing. Inside, he set down his dark, sodden instrument bag, left it dripping on a sidetable in the front hall, went upstairs and changed out of his soaked clothes and then had a lunch of venison sausage and rice, and at last he called for John.

"We are going for a ride, John," he told the six-year-old boy. "And we may get wet."

The storm did not slacken in the early afternoon. The woods were dripping, noisy with pelting, driving rain, so that the boy now riding forward of his uncle on the doctor's sleek charcoal mare could scarcely hear the man's commands to the horse. He saw other people abroad even in this weather, some trudging along on foot under the weight of heavy, sopping coats, some on horses, some on saddle mules. No one was moving quickly through the deluge, yet all were going forth purposefully, as if to the same place for the same reason. As the Ellerslie road neared the main road down into Fayetteville, John saw small groups of soldiers in uniform, boys not much older than he, grown men and even a few old ones, too, out in all this weather.

Later on, John Maffitt would hear much more of this day, from his uncle and his aunt and from almost everyone he would meet with them in the city—about the troops that had gathered in town to be reviewed, about all the women in full fine dress to see and be seen, one banquet right after another from early evening till after midnight and even the next morning. And about the endless touring of the new hotel that had barely been finished in time.

When the Maffitts reached the main road, John craned to see the stern, pleased face of his uncle walking the mare up under a great longleaf that towered over the turkey oak and scrub, the wiregrass floor of the woods. They did not dismount. John stared both ways up and down the highway at other men and boys on horse and on foot nearly lining the way, like a parade route in a town, though this place was miles away yet from the city. Over on the other side of the road, another boy held aloft an American flag, and when he lowered it and it hung straight out, John Maffitt counted the stars, four rows of six. The rain weakened at last, stalled for a spell into a drizzle, and he heard a piercing fife's whistle and the muffled beat from a tom-tom up the way.

An hour went by. The rain picked back up. A second hour passed, the rain holding steady.

Sometimes he could still make out the fife, if not its tune, but most times he could not hear over the rain. Suddenly there came shouts from off to the north, *huzzah*s and *hear-hear*s, and long crooning wails and outright short chops, yells hunters make when calling in dogs, or urging them on in the woods, and it all grew louder. Doctor Maffitt leaned down to John, squeezing his shoulders, saying: "Now we will see him."

Presently a dark coach pulled by four roan stallions rolled into view, and an older man peered forth from the small side aperture, nodding, smiling, waving, saying something indecipherable over the noise of the rain and the horses' hooves and the carriage wheels, though it would have been indecipherable in any event, for the old man's well-wishes and salutations were all in French. The shouts and long wails picked up off to their right, and John, waving vigorously as the carriage passed by not twelve feet away, believed he had caught the old man's eye, his smile, and the boy said breathlessly to his uncle: "Who is he? Who is that?"

Doctor Maffitt regarded his nephew, his ward, and grinned, for he had not till now told John what this rain-soaked ride and wait were all about.

"That man," he said, "is a hero of the Revolution." And he let out an uncharacteristic yell of his own, a following cry intended to hurry the coach and its heroic occupant on, and then he continued: "That is the Marquis de Lafayette, who saved the day in the war," the doctor said. "Major-General Lafayette—and now you've seen him, and you can tell your children . . ."

"My children?"

". . . and grandchildren some day. That you saw him right up close, so close you could've almost reached out and touched him." Turning his charcoal mare once again to the wet, darkening woods, Doctor Maffitt said, "And now we can go home."

White Plains, New York

Not long after crossing the broad Hudson River on a ferry, well up the valley from New York, the young boy from Cumberland County, North Carolina, arrived in the village of White Plains by way of Westchester County's overland stage. *Enough of dust, enough of mud, enough of tipsy drivers and their four-in-hand teams of tired horses.*

John Maffitt had been sent North by his uncle to attend the new White Plains Academy, a preparatory school under the direction of Professor John Swinburne, master of arts, Wesleyan University. Amidst the elms and maples on the North Broadway common that the school fronted upon, the professor and his boys were out playing ball, but they stopped their game and walked over and gathered round to greet the stagecoach. When the coach door opened, they gazed upon this small curiosity from the South who climbed down and presented himself. And then they peppered and pelted him with questions.

"What's your name, then?"

"John Newland Maffitt."

"Why are you so dusty and muddy?"

"Been traveling for over a week, had to help push the stage out of mudholes."

"Why do you talk so strangely?"

"I was going to ask you all the same thing."

"Do you own slaves?"

"No, but I know folks who do."

"Tell us something special about yourself, John," said Professor Swinburne.

"I was born at sea," John Maffitt replied at once. He was very proud of this indeed, and declaring it forthrightly, cheerfully, made him smile among strangers, and, as this was special and fresh, the boys were immediately taken with him, and they lit up and liked him. Till one older boy queried: "Is that it? Is there nothing else?"

"Well, yessir, there is," John Maffitt said. "I saw Lafayette."

At this word, the schoolboys roared, thoroughly disarmed, and swarmed the new boy, clapping him upon his shoulders, shaking his hand, for they had all studied the Revolution and they all knew of Lafayette, though not a one of them ever laid eyes on him nor knew anyone else who had—till now. They erupted in cheers and *huzzahs*, and competed for who would lead him to the small brick dormitory, to his room and its bunkbed.

Here at the Academy John Maffitt would find marvels and wonders: a cabinet filled with minerals, little bits of copper and iron and gold and silver and more, and a library boasting a thousand books, home to both Lochinvar and Rip Van Winkle. Here he would study reading, penmanship, composition, history; the ancient languages of Rome and Athens; the modern Romance languages of Italy, France, and Spain. Here he would learn geography and geometry, trigonometry and astronomy.

And, above all, surveying and navigation. He would love these subjects almost with abandon—their globes and maps and charts, their tools, the compass, the sextant, telescope, all their words and language, metes and bounds, chains, leagues, fathoms, knots.

He would learn of Phoenicians. He would read Homer. He would hear of the *wine-dark* sea.

This was what White Plains held in store for him. Now, on his first day, his new comrades left him in his new room regarding his bed and gravely considering where to put his small trunk. They told him of dinner—beef stew tonight—across the small quad in the mess hall they pointed out to him through the window, warning him about six o'clock sharp and advising him how to catch the time from the town-hall clock and its quarter-hour bells. John Newland Maffitt was nine years old, and after these many days journeying north the ticket his uncle had bought him was still pinned to his jacket.

Aboard the *St. Louis*

Pensacola, Florida, and Caribbean Sea

1832–1834

On February 25, 1832, three days past his thirteenth birthday, John Maffitt received at White Plains an official appointment from President Andrew Jackson: the boy was going to become an acting midshipman in the U.S. Navy.

Perhaps this was all somehow the Reverend Maffitt's doing—John's father, now a well-known and increasingly popular touring preacher, knew the President personally, and he knew from John's uncle at Ellerslie how well John Maffitt had been doing at White Plains, how taken the youth was with mathematics in all its forms, in the Euclidean beauty of geometry, and in the cold hard precision of graphs and charts. However this had come to pass, the boy was enthralled, and, though he had thrived in the New York academy, he left and did not look back.

In early August 1832, he reported to the deep-water naval station at Pensacola in the Florida panhandle, there to join the *St. Louis*, a seven-hundred-ton sloop of war, and to start patrolling the Caribbean Sea, the coasts of Cuba and Puerto Rico, and the Sir Francis Drake Channel through the Virgin Islands, where the magnificent frigatebird led the way. He received his first uniform, tried it on, stood before a mirror and saw himself—chalk-white pants and brass buttons up the front of a dark blue coat. He liked the look of the U.S. Navy and thus saw, as best a thirteen-year-old boy could, the look of his life. He was ready for all of it, ready to do the midshipman's tasks, running orders from one officer to the next and thereby having the run of the ship, ready to learn what captain and chaplain and the creaking of cordage and spars all had to teach him, ready to see the world from the water's side.

Acting Midshipman Maffitt longed to be happy, completely happy, yet even at this great new moment he could not quite be so.

His sister, Ann C. Maffitt, named after their mother, had died of cholera that past summer while attending a boarding school on Broadway in New York City. A relative sent John the new Boston periodical that published "My Child," a poetic eulogy his father wrote while in New Haven, honoring the dead girl and ending:

But we shall meet above
To part again no more,
Where blooms my angel love
Upon that blest shore.

Reverend Maffitt's poem appeared in the pages of *The Liberator*—an abolitionist publication—and on the sloop the *St. Louis*, on Sundays sometimes when the crew was at leisure, John Maffitt brought the magazine with him from his quarters up to the bow rail and read the poem's twenty-four lines aloud to himself and the sea, and in this way he mourned her death and did not forget her. And as he sorted through the chambers of his heart, he heard *my angel love* as the phrase echoed about, and he wondered what his sister was really like, his mother's namesake, what she studied at the school in the city and beyond that what she had wanted of the world, and he wondered no less what his father, the preacher and poet, was like. He found plenty enough in all this to sift, for all the Sundays that fall, as he would for many a Sunday yet to come.

Back in Pensacola in early December, John Maffitt went into the little city and promptly encountered a friend from Fayetteville, and this incidental fact alone made him rhapsodize of home. The *St. Louis* did not linger long in port but sailed back out for nearly all of 1833, and Maffitt, fourteen, walked the streets of Havana, Cuba, for the first time in his life and there, also for the first time, felt the warmth of young women's dark eyes upon him.

When he returned to Pensacola in late January 1834, he received an extended leave ashore. He journeyed at once to Ellerslie up in Cumberland County, North Carolina, where he had longed to be and where—to his beloved cousin Eliza as well as to anyone else at home who would listen—Acting Midshipman Maffitt now had very much in the way of tales to tell.

Grandy, Early 1820s – 1832

Camden and Pasquotank Counties, North Carolina

EARLY 1820S

For a short time Captain Grandy commanded Enoch Sawyer's shingle-getters in the Great Dismal Swamp. But then reversals in the Norfolk businesses of his sons forced Sawyer to cover their losses and cut back on his own operations in the swamp and concentrate instead on his riverside plantation in southern Camden County.

Moses Grandy, a boatman for years, suddenly found himself a field hand again, poorly rationed as all of Sawyer's field hands were, baking in the broad cut-and-drained lands from sunup to sundown, spring through fall. Potatoes, cabbage, beans, and corn. This was a far harder life than his life on the water had been, and he suffered for it—he suffered the punitive power of Brooks the overseer, the worst one Grandy had ever encountered, a man of such malicious indifference he would flog a new mother till her blood and her milk ran together on her chest.

Moses Grandy implored Enoch Sawyer to give his field hands more food, on the grounds that they might work better for him, and Grandy gained the concession.

Then one Sunday morning, Grandy approached the porch of Sawyer's big house on the river, where he and Mrs. Sawyer were sitting and rocking, and he further implored Sawyer to allow him to buy his freedom yet again, and once again for six hundred dollars.

Both of the Sawyers burst out laughing at him.

"Why, our friend the captain put a thousand dollars on the table for you just a few nights ago, and we wouldn't accept it," said Sawyer, who turned to his wife. "I think Moses is quite drunk to propose such a thing, don't you, my dear?"

Mrs. Sawyer, laughing still, shook her head, said nothing, and rose and walked into the house.

First thing Monday Moses Grandy reappeared at the big house and announced to Enoch Sawyer that he would not go to the fields anymore. He said he intended to walk to Norfolk and get Moses Myers or one of the other merchants for whom he had captained to buy him from Sawyer. Of a different mind this morning, Sawyer sat and signed a note, *to whom it may concern*, advising the reader that he would accept six hundred dollars for Grandy, and then handed the paper over to the black man.

Moses Grandy was away at once.

He strode with full purpose up to Camden village, then miles north to Burnt Mills, and on to South Mills where the last locks were on the Dismal Swamp Canal, and then on up the canalbank past Major Farange's Tavern at the Old Brick House, past the Virginia state boundary line and the Feeder Ditch up to the lake, past Northwest River, and past all the locks. When he finally arrived very late at Deep Creek, the canal's northern end, he stopped for water, for food if they had it, at the home of friends—Captain Edward Minner and his wife, Quakers who, upon hearing Moses Grandy's mission, told him he need go no farther. "Stop here for the night," Captain Minner said. "We will go to Sawyer and buy you with rusty coins we've got buried out back, and then let you buy your freedom from us, for lock-solid certain this time."

Tuesday now: Captain Minner and Captain Grandy on horseback rode down to Major Farange's Tavern, two and a half miles south of the Virginia line, Grandy betting that Sawyer would have come there to do business, which he had. Enoch Sawyer was there in Major Farange's to get himself out of the canal business, there to sell his shares in the Dismal Swamp Canal and be done with it. He had no way of knowing where Moses Grandy had gone or what he had been about since he quit the fields Monday morning and walked away from Sawyer's plantation on the Pasquotank, carrying on him the paper Sawyer had signed.

Within the tavern it was dim, smoky, aromatic of tobacco and cheese, fish and ale. When Sawyer saw Grandy walk in with Captain Minner, he was not surprised, for Grandy's years on the canal-boats had put him in touch with many a mariner up and down the Carolina and Virginia waterways. But when he heard what Grandy and Minner had concocted he was taken aback, and he had a ready answer: "No. The last thing I promised Mrs. Sawyer before I left the river this morning was that I would not sell Moses." Sawyer alleged that his wife wanted Moses Grandy back on the Sawyer place, but Minner pressed him quickly, sharply, holding Sawyer's paper from the day before, asking him loudly: "Is this letter not in your handwriting? Are you not a man of your word?"

"Yes, it is," Sawyer answered. "And you know I am a man of honor."

"Well, then, I'll buy him," said Minner, and then more broadly to the men gathered at Farange's, to the room at large: "And he'll have his freedom once he's paid me back—and I'll not charge him a cent of interest for it. I'll have no Negro slave dragging me down to hell!"

Still Sawyer refused.

The men grumbled. They liked Captain Grandy, and they—like everyone else in six counties across northeastern North Carolina—knew he had been cheated twice already. Most men wanted to see another man get what he had earned. Yet Enoch Sawyer was not without a stubborn bearing; he was also collector of customs in Camden, and they all knew, too, they had to deal with him. And they all knew that not too long ago he had entertained the President of the United States at his home, that Sawyer's pretty daughter had played airs on her harp for President Monroe and brought him a bouquet of roses to boot. Sawyer could withstand a little social pressure when it came to nothing more than the matter of a slave, for God's sake, and so he held firm.

Until the Scotsman Wiley McPherson spoke.

This was the marrying man known to all as Squire Wiley, the man to whom eloping Virginia couples came in droves for quick hitchings and his blessings upon them, the man whose last name everyone pronounced "Make-fashion." As an overseer in canal-building work, McPherson had many hired-out slaves under his command working in water, mud, and muck that they later slept upon as best they could—he was well and widely known in these parts as a man who was hard on slaves. The men there at Farange's ordinary witnessing all this would sooner have expected kindness and forebearance toward Africans from hyenas than they would have from the squire, who now lined out his words slowly and sternly. "As often as Moses has bought his freedom, Enoch," Squire Wiley said, "he ought to go free."

Grandy was even more astonished than his owner, and, feeling his life held during this moment in some strange kind of balance, he repeated in his mind those words that just fell from Squire Willie's lips, thinking maybe some sort of canalbank miracle was occurring: *He has never been known to speak up for a colored man before.*

Enoch Sawyer was too political—his friend in the White House, his brother Lemuel in Congress—to resist the moment the Fates had woven together here at Farange's ordinary. To stand down the Quaker who held a paper Enoch himself had signed was one thing, but to go against the popular Squire Wiley's judgment before all these witnesses, that was too much—by word of mouth, he would lose respect across the district, and it would cost him and his family votes, no doubt about it or way around it. His resolve collapsed, and in a few moments the dingy coins Captain Minner had dug up out of the Virginia earth fell from Minner's hands into Sawyer's, and Sawyer signed Moses Grandy over to Captain Minner and the deed was done.

Moses had his fourth new owner in four years. This man, he knew, was the one who would set him free at last.

Lake Drummond, Virginia
Great Dismal Swamp
EARLY 1820S

Now some of Moses Grandy's comrades from freightboat days took him up to the lake, where he could live and rest and heal for a while from rheumatism, making the trip up the Feeder Ditch with him in the middle of a juniper skiff and one man fore and one aft, paddling like all get-out, and a third man above them on the path than ran along the ditch, pulling them forward with a long hemp towrope.

They had seen and felt the water rushing at them as they came across the main canal and entered the ditch and knew it would be a long hard go to make it to the lake and then across it to where a lean-to camp awaited the ailing Grandy. There would be no gliding over the water, as there often was in the big ditch, only a repeated digging and beating on, one pull after the next, the towman too leaning shoulders down into his work. A hurricane the week before had flooded the lowlands, filling the cypress creeks and the peat grounds on the Dismal's west side, and now it was draining rapidly out of Lake Drummond and through the spillway gates and over them, too, and the dark brown waters were frothy with foam thick and bright as spindrift on a seabeach. It kept coming at the little craft with the anxious force of a headwaters stream, and the men worked ceaselessly, their boat against that current, bearing them upward to the bright lake in the middle of the thousand-square-mile swamp.

Captain Grandy could do little to help his men, strong as he was, and it grated upon him, ground at him, as he saw how hard they were digging at the dark water and felt how little forward motion they made with each pull at the paddles. He was used to being the strongest, the gamest, the worthiest in all matters of strength and endurance, but not now, not this day of our Lord. He was no invalid, though, not by nature or spirit, and knew he must retrieve all his strength, get it back and tamp it up solid into himself and be no man's patient ever again. He was used to being the depend-upon for so many, and he must be that again.

Must be.

A small patch of October blue sat far ahead of them, just above the water in a vanishing point a mile or more yet away. *We must have gone three miles by now*, Grandy wished, though he knew they had gone but two. In another hour, midafternoon, they would wind up near the spillway and drag themselves and the boat up the steep, ten-foot bank to the lake level. After only a few moments of rest and bread and water, they would be off again, without the towman now, for there was only the impenetrable, illimitable swamp off to either side of the upper Feeder Ditch and no path for him. The current still ran hard against them, and Moses felt the whole wet wilderness draining right by them, water wanting its great way out to the sea and wanting to push the men out along with it. In a quarter hour the little boat with the three black men in it reached the lake, the swamp's highest point, its jewel.

Cypress trees hundreds of years old stood in the shallow lake waters, which washed through their roots and over their brown burnished knees. Shores near and far reflected perfectly in the lake's pure, flat-calm surface, a reduplication of the cypress around them and the far-off blue woods and the high-piled white clouds in blue skies above that made all three of them gasp, witnessing without shame the natural glory and handiwork all about them.

"Lord God," said one.

Then they bent to their task once more, Moses Grandy staring sternly at the warped and illusory curve, the passing strange vision of Drummond's far shore, and sternly staring out toward the spot where the lean-to lay that would be his new home for a while. They got him to the appointed spot just before dusk, leaving him alone with enough flour and grits, Irish potatoes, and salt pork for a couple of weeks and promising him to return with more food and blankets soon, well before first frost.

"You all right, Cap'n?"

"Yes, you all head on now. I'll be fine. See you."

"See you, too, Cap'n."

And then he watched after them. He watched the small craft pushing off from shore, as the men pulled and dug and as it crept and drifted away from him, cleaving the lake's surface and trailing a line of divide behind, till the boat seemed no larger than the line it created, till the nearly full harvest moon rose slowly, grandly above him at least half as large as the great lake itself, till the brown barred owls, those faraway and those close by, felt the crisp night coming on and rose to it and let loose their echoing, cascading, querying serenade *Who cooks for you all?* upon the moonlit lakewaters before him, into the juniper and cypress wilds all around him, and straight across his strong and lonesome heart.

Dawn, and the day was clean. Moses Grandy sat up in front of his lean-to on the southwest shore, still awakening in the fresh October morning chill and now fixing his mind on the abject need to get a fire going. He stared out into a deep morning silence over lake and swamp that was almost palpable, a quiet before the men in the shingle camps well north of him woke and went to work, when he would hear them talking as familiarly as if they were only a few dozen yards away, because that was the way sound carried in such deep, flat woods, and he would hear the carboys and their carts and the small mules drawing them over the narrow log-corduroy roads laid down in the swamp's mud.

The water of Lake Drummond was flat, calm, and black as the Egyptian darkness, he thought, holding himself against the cold and against the rheumatism born of his many years of just such mornings. Briefly he brooded over Egypt and another people in bondage in another time—and another Moses. As the daylight came coolly on, he saw first one, then two, then more: sleeping swans loosely flocked on the lake before him, and then the eastern sun suddenly coursed at him over top of the rust-gold cypress and deep green cedars of the far shore, two miles distant, and the top rim of the sun shot a fire into the lake mists and plated the very waters at his feet with gold.

Sitting here, reflected Moses Grandy, *I am free. Yet my wife at Enoch Sawyer's in Camden—where this black water is bound, down the Pasquotank River—is not. Nor my young son. If not for them I could stay here and rest till I have healed myself, and then vanish into the woods behind me, just like so many others have. Yet that's a wretched life, I know—and why trade one wretchedness for another? I can't stop trying, not now. If I ever do it'd be just like my brother, lying down in leaves and waiting for buzzards to come rip me apart.*

I can set down here till I feel better. Swamp Company slaves bringing me food, what little I need. Some days I can pull the rive

on some juniper and get a few shingles, maybe a few barrel staves.
I can stay here and heal if it takes a year. . . . Then I can work the
canalboats a couple years more, if that's what it takes to pay back
Captain Minner and Mrs. Minner.
Put more wood on the fire. This is October, man. Call it the fall.
Guide the boats again when you can.
Work on.
If that's what it takes to be free.

Firewood he pitched onto the lean-to fire kicked up sparks and thunked just loudly enough to spook the swans, which squawked and yawped and flapped and then, coursing low over the lake's black water, flew on away.

Atlantic Ocean

CIRCA 1826–1827

After a year in the Great Dismal, Moses Grandy put in three more years back on the canalboats, and he settled his debt. Duly repaid, Captain and Mrs. Minner set Moses Grandy free.

For the first couple of months of his freedom, Grandy went up to live in Providence, Rhode Island, to get established and known as a free man (Captain Minner's plan for him), but he was homesick and soon sailed back home to see his wife. Captain Minner encouraged him to venture north again, and so he signed on as an able-bodied, blue-water seaman, at work on packet boats that now ran regularly between Philadelphia and New York, and coastwise up and down the eastern seaboard of America, some even to Liverpool, England. The packets were deep-draft, three-masted square-riggers, with side-wheel paddles driven by steam, and they were moving everything America needed: sars of bricks, planks of lumber, bales of cotton, casks of lime, chunks of marble, sugar, flour, rum, the works.

Moses Grandy was strong again, more willing and happier at his work than ever before, because if he knew anything well by now it was water and freight, and because his work and his pay was finally his own and not half or three-quarters some other man's. These big packets were a far cry from the homely canal-boats that had gained him his liberty, and ocean swells and mountainous seas and waves breaking over decks were something else again. Yet he pondered goods and men and markets and knew what he was about and he knew, too, that only the crafts and the ports and what goods were belowdecks were truly new, and that men were all in all the same as ever.

Boston, Massachusetts

LATE 1820S

Very early on Sunday morning, September 2, 1827, at his house not on the canal but in the town of Norfolk at the corner of Church and Freemason Streets, after a brief illness Edward Minner died. His wife and daughter mourned him and lamented the loss of the man they had always found kind and indulgent. So, too, did Moses Grandy, whose life had changed course by the grace of Captain Minner. Upon learning of Minner's death, he knew that his sponsor and his main protector in the South was gone.

Captain Grandy then fetched up in the great port of Boston, the peninsula with its wharves all fingered out into the harbor like spokes, tucked well in from the sea behind a slew of islands, and there in its world of muscles and labor he found his place, among the slogging housewrights, painters and printers, drain diggers and distillers, shoemakers, coachmakers, bakers and whipmakers, leather finishers with tannin on their wares and in their skin, stablekeepers, measurers and mariners, gravers, and all the many widows of a seaport town. As he must, the tall black man went forth working around and about the port's vast docks and wharves: now a stevedore, now a sawyer pulling his end of a crosscut saw or sawing with a whipsaw, now a sooty shoveler wheelbarrowing coal.

But Grandy was far more waterman than longshoreman, and he lasted only a while on land before going to sea again.

Atlantic Ocean

CIRCA 1830

Moses Grandy shipped out with Captain Cobb to Puerto Rico on the 73-foot, 103-ton Boston schooner *New Packet*—the same small ship that, after a storm tore her up coming home from

Boston Harbor, from the ship house at the west end of the Navy Yard

Grenada, had laid up in Elizabeth City for three months' over-
haul in 1827. As they sailed into St. John's under the commanding Fortress del Morro, its thick tawny brick walls almost a part of
the cliffside, from the portside bow rail he regarded a figure high
up above in a watchtower's turret, who in turn was watching him.
The *New Packet* was showing her colors, and she brought trade
and bore no arms. Here among the Spanish and the refugees from
the wars in Europe and what was left of the Indians, the American
ship was welcome.

Puerto Rico was a huge, fecund island. Emigrés from Spain
had been buying out small farmers, or driving them out with land
grants from the king in Madrid, making tenants of those who only
last year had been small landowners, and independent. These
poor, free *jíbaros* worked the new plantations alongside Afri-

can slaves, and the land put out, and the port was rich enough to be worthy of its name. A little east of St. John's, Grandy learned, was a small town called Carolina. Though most of the people of color whom he saw in the city streets and at the wharf were free, he heard of the slave gangs that worked the plantations in the countryside not so far from the port, and he quickly found the place achingly reminiscent of his own Carolina.

To the docks flowed a steady stream of oxen yoked in pairs pulling high-wheeled carts, some piled high with huge jute bags full of coffeebeans, others hauling thirty-gallon barrels of sugar. Down to the quay and up alongside the ship glided the swaying carts. Men rolled the 120-pound barrels up the *New Packet*'s gangplank, along the deck, and on down into the hold, where big bags of coffee would soon lie atop them.

"How long we in this place?" Moses Grandy asked Captain Cobb.

"Overnight," the captain said. "Just long enough to load and go."

"Yes, sir, Captain," said Moses. "Load and go."

Yet the work did not go quite so quickly, for the *New Packet* had come into St. John's during Carnaval, and many dockworkers were not working at all. They were roaming the streets wearing masks, bright red devil's heads or toothy donkey's heads, even a gorilla with seven horns and blue about his eyes, all these sharp horns curving skyward, the roaming men both frightening and thrilling small children who shrieked with strange delight as the roamers struck at them with inflated bladders and warned them of ghosts and demons and dangers lurking just around that corner there. Not understanding their street cries, their Spanish, Moses Grandy walked among them like a hypnotized stranger, marveling at so many people wandering free and shouting and singing and playing music—some banging on rum-barrel *bomba* drums and some shaking maracas, some raking a many-tined and rasping pick like a woman's comb across a grooved, ridged gourd, others over a piece of wood, a guiro, making everywhere a high-speed ticking, the sound of time racing away.

Grandy grasped what they were about. Older children taunted the devil figures and women waved backhandedly at them. A donkey brayed at a devil and danced around him. Moses Grandy stopped and stared up a St. John's street away from the docks at all the knots and tangles of Puerto Ricans as they meandered and danced fervently around a dozen devils, laughing at death. I have done that, too, he judged, in my own way. Though he was but mildly amused by the street-theater battle raging between good and evil, life and death, he knew it was his fight, too, no less than theirs, and he did not begrudge them their spirited fun.

Moses Grandy walked on, weaving in and among the devils dancing. He was much taller than most of the Puerto Ricans, and he sensed the admiring gazes of women as he passed. He missed his wife keenly, and with images of her much in his mind, he left the Carnaval and returned to his ship.

Nearly seventeen hundred miles of open ocean, a sail of several weeks, lay between St. John's and Boston. The *New Packet* caught a ride north on the Gulf Stream and made good speed even in light wind. Off Massachusetts, though, when Captain Cobb turned west-northwest, standing for Boston, the winds turned on him—the schooner, giving too much leeway, was blown landward by a strong nor'easter.

The *New Packet* did not clear Cape Cod but instead was driven in upon the Nauset Bars, site of countless wrecks.

Moses Grandy and his fellows on the schooner tried, with every letup of the wind, to kedge their craft off these shoals and right her and sail on. Even these stout-hearted seamen were no match for the North Atlantic in late winter, though, and, after struggling vainly for a good long while, they all heard Captain Cobb's order to abandon ship and get ashore, and so they did.

At the cliffs near Eastham they came in, and now, exhausted and cold and soaked, they had to climb sand mountains and march overland through sandy terrain, bare but for poverty-grass. Captain Cobb had many friends among the sea captains who made their homes in the village of Dennis on Cape Cod Bay, and here he and Grandy and the others would find succor and, soon, a packet across the bay and back to Boston.

Sometime later, Grandy learned, the *New Packet* was pulled off the bars and recovered by other men, a fate more felicitous than that of most ships foundering upon the cape. He had worked the water all his life, nary a mishap until now. How many chances did a mariner get? Chances to swim and walk away from a shipwreck. How many times could a man dance a ring or two around death, like those Puerto Ricans, and laugh at Old Scratch? He knew full well that he had just done that dance.

Yet Moses Grandy did not laugh.

African Meeting House

Belknap Street, Boston, Massachusetts

JANUARY 6, 1832

Over the streets of Beacon Hill Moses Grandy strode, on his way to a gathering that men told him he must not miss. A merciless nor'easter lashed Boston, with rain and hail comingled fiercely falling and snow falling fiercely with them, too. Old Christmas, Twelfth Night, Epiphany, Holy Day, Grandy thought. And what would come of it?

Down Belknap Street, he approached the redbrick, three-story building, its four tall, curved-top windows filled with lamplight. Several men, one with a pipe lit and smoke rising thinly, huddled near the front door. Too cold for this, he thought, yet he nodded at them and stopped and lifted his gaze, wishing he could make out the writing above the door.   "African," the man with the pipe said solemnly, seeing Moses Grandy squinting at the chiseled words.

"African?" says Grandy. "What does it say?"

"'Cato Gardner,'" the man intoned. "'First Promoter of this Building 1806.' He was African."

"Are you part of this tonight?" Grandy asked.

"Yes," he said. "And you are, too. Go on in."

Inside, Moses Grandy climbed the steep stairs into the second-story sanctuary, a big open hall with curved walls. Reminds me of a periauger, he thought. Reminds me of a boat back home. To reach the high gallery he pulled upon the dark, almost vertical banister and climbed the steep steps. The room was not a church but was like a church, big and open and not much warmer than

African Meeting House, Boston

the street. Moses took his seat at the end of a bench and waited and watched as the African Meeting House filled up, mostly with black people, some of whom he knew from the Second Ward or the docks. When the hall was nearly full a few white men (twelve of them, like apostles, Moses Grandy thought), dressed formally, entered and headed toward seats at the fore that seemed to have been saved for them, and sat down rigid and severe. The last of them was a balding young man of medium build with a large nose and small pair of glasses resting across it; before sitting, he regarded those in the hall and acknowledged them.

The man from outside with the pipe now entered and closed the door behind him with a strong, purposeful push that sent a clap through the room, like that of a judge banging a gavel for order. Then he strode to the oak lectern and spoke, and, even though Moses Grandy could not hear him very well, he knew the man was praying. This leader gestured toward the white people, pointed at one, and the young balding man stood and walked to the fore.

"Who is that man?" Grandy asked the heavily shawled woman beside him.

"He's the man puts out *The Liberator*," she said. "Mister William Lloyd Garrison. Just you listen."

"Well, who is he then?"

"He's why you're here," she said. "Why we all here."

Mister Garrison, thin and wearing slender oval, wire-framed glasses, held the lectern and stood for a few moments, gathering himself. What hair he had hung from the lower half of his skull. With his sharp nose and his black vest and frock coat and black cravat collaring him, he had, thought Moses Grandy, the look of a country preacher. Once Garrison opened his mouth and spoke, though, Grandy knew he had never heard or seen a preacher quite like this one, not a white one or a black one, either.

The man's voice had a fire in it and a cold fury, too. He was so young, in his mid-twenties, Grandy reckoned, full of energy, wound tight. He said he would publish *The Liberator* and that he would keep sleeping on his office floor, as he had done for one year and one week now, until victory, if that was what it took. Until

William Lloyd Garrison, editor of The Liberator

there was no more slavery in the land. Discomfort was nothing to him. Fatigue was nothing to him. Only the Lord's truth mattered, and he would stand alone with it, if need be, and await the results, and he would work for it until it triumphed and abided. He would work till he was tired, yet he would tire not. He could not rest until the last man or woman or child in chains was set free. He wanted that to happen tonight, here in Boston, here in this country, here in this New England, and if that freedom did not come to each and every man, down to the last man, tonight, he would say tomorrow, even more firmly, that it must happen today. No Christian should rest. Not one person who spoke Jesus's name and claimed Him, not one, should delay for a single moment but should speak and act to set his brethren free. Immediately. At once. Now. Is not each of us, the free, the enslaved, a child of God? Of course we are all his children, of course we are! No chains, no shackles, no whips, no auction blocks, no degradation, and moral outrage upon all who touch the wretched institution, no human bondage for anyone ever, ever again!

"Amen," said Moses Grandy, loudly, as loud as any of the black men and women near him. "Amen!"

Mister Garrison stopped and lowered his gaze. He was only looking for a glass of water, which someone offered him, but he seemed like a man in a trance. This was Garrison, printer's devil, abandoned as a child by his New Brunswick sea-captain father, Abijah, raised by his pious mother, Frances Maria. But he was also, he knew, the modern evocation of the ancient Greek Aristides the Just—and blessed is the just man, who walketh in his integrity.

"Tonight, my friends," Mister Garrison said (and if it was with joy it was a cold joy, his voice secure in his purposefulness), "in this hallowed hall, we are founding a society to propound and deliver this great good work. We are founding the New England Anti-Slavery Society."

He had barely said the words, the name, before thunderous applause shook the African Meeting House, and everyone in this roomful of black Americans stood and all stamped their feet in defiance and approval.

"Say it with me," Mister Garrison implored them all.

"The New England Anti-Slavery Society."

The choral words poured forth not as a cheer, or a chant, but as a declaration, a pledge, a solemn oath. There was much agitation in the room, and when the meeting drew to a close, William Lloyd Garrison was thronged. Everyone wished to meet and speak with him.

"What can we do to help?"

"I will bring you wood."

"I can patch that place on your coat."

"Where is your office, maybe I can sweep it out for you sometime."

Moses Grandy had to brush away tears, nor was he alone in this. He was looking through the crowd, catching glimpses of Mister Garrison, but what he saw was a black woman in a wagon on a road running beside a long, dark canal hundreds of miles and many years away from this place and this moment.

At the end, the crowd poured out onto the narrow street, where shoes and boots were quickly soaked by the slush, and all who were there witnessed William Lloyd Garrison stopping and touching one hand to the brick building's side and pointing with the other up toward the heart of Boston, declaring to his followers and to the fierce, storming heavens: "My friends, we have met tonight in this obscure schoolhouse, but before many years we will rock Faneuil Hall!"

Captain Grandy had been among the last that night to get to the fore and shake Mister Garrison's hand.

Aboard the *James Maury*

JANUARY–SEPTEMBER 1832

Once more, boys, once more, go to sea once more.
A man must be blind to make up his mind to go to sea once
more.

To the Mediterranean Sea Moses Grandy had sailed twice, and now he was going to the East Indies, at long last to the other side of the earth. He shipped out on the *James Maury* to Batavia in Java, Captain Woodbury at the helm, outbound from Boston on January 19, 1832.

Moses Grandy stood at the James Maury's port rail—most all his fellow sailors did—as she slowly glided out, and he looked back at the USS *Constitution*, the Navy's great frigate, listening to the workmen who had for months been refitting her, getting the hog out of her keel, as they cried out to each other and hammered on, replacing decking, recaulking her, replacing the broken window lights in the captain's quarters aft and glazing them.

She was a massive three-master, yet Grandy thought there was something sleek about her, too, her long black hull below the long white stripe of gunports, great iron cannon lurking behind each one, and, high above, her yardarms, each seeming nearly as broad as a *James Maury* mast was tall.

He noted the old warship's complex rigging, a webwork supplied by the ropewalks of New England, and he thought of how many men's lives had crossed upon her decks over the years, for he knew she was built and launched back in the '90s. *Lord God,* Moses Grandy reflected, *that ship, she is near about old as I am, and been all around just like me. Just like me and then some.*

Soon, as they pulled eastward across the harbor, past the rock islands and sand spits and out into Boston Bay, they were unfurling canvas and laying out more sail. The *James Maury* was under way, and a seaman best attend to his tasks and keep his mind right upon them.

––––––––

The *James Maury*, a 394-ton ship built in Boston in 1825, was already a storied vessel by the time Moses Grandy joined her crew. Under Captain Woodbury, she had sailed the year after she was launched down to Havana, Cuba, and from there stood for St. Petersburg, Russia, and was spoken in the Gulf of Finland the 2nd of August, 1826, on her way into Cronstadt. The week before Christmas, 1826, the fruits of her sail were on display back in Boston, where Josiah Bradlee & Company, 34 India Street down near the water—the same merchant who in other times touted in the *Boston Commercial Gazette* such disparate wares as English Bleaching Powder and summer-strained lamp oil and sperm candles, and scores of pipefuls of cognac (both Seignette's and Rasteau's) from La Rochelle—invited the public's attention to all he now had to show from the recent landing of the *James Maury*: Chlebnikoff's sail cloth, Ravcus Duck, and walnut brown Flemish cloth, nearly fifteen hundred pieces in all.

The year 1827 was not so kind to the *James Maury* or her master. Sailing north, two weeks out of Havana, a zealous nor'easter galed down upon her. The ship lay to, her main topsail close reefed. At 10:00 P.M. a heavy sea broke over the ship, washing away everything loose on deck, and carrying off the second mate and three able-bodied seamen, all lost at sea. The captain was slammed across the deck, his arm broken above the elbow, his head gashed three times, and his body bruised black and blue. The first mate got the captain back to his cabin, ordered the ship's pumps to work, and at 5:00 A.M. the next morning found the ship still had four and a half feet of water in her hold. Twelve hours later, the men had cleared the water and all hands were at work on repair, for the *James Maury*'s sails had been blown away. The mate and another sailor set the captain's arm as best they could and dressed his wounds. On March 27, when the great spring storm was spent, the crew bent new sails and the voyage proceeded. Gales kept beating upon them all the rest of the voyage, and on May 4 they arrived at last in Elsineur, where they were in quarantine for four days. The captain, noted the first mate in a letter to the *Salem Gazette*, had been in bed for forty-three days and feared he would lose his arm. In print, the mate regarded this voyage of the *James Maury* as "tedious."

Yet in early 1828 she cleared Boston under Captain Woodbury, bound again for Cuba and Europe, a tour she would repeat in 1829. During 1831 and 1832, after the five-year Java War ended, the *James Maury* would be outward bound for even farther pavilions, for the wide-open Dutch markets on the Java Sea. Moses Grandy had been eager to make one of these East Indies trips— Captain Woodbury and the *James Maury* were taking him to the other side of the world, for one thing, and, for another, he would finally earn enough to secure his future happiness upon their return.

This was the rich, high time of the East India trade, when America's merchantmen and mariners plied around the Horn, paying call at Ceylon and Cochin for cinnamon and pepper, at Hong Kong for deep red and black silks and China tea sets and basins and plates with old blue men portrayed fishing or praying at ponds and beside rivers and at peace with the world, for nankeen and duck and curtain-cloth and lacquered cabinets for the Yankee home. The *James Maury* would call upon the island empire that the Dutch had come up out of their own fens and marshes to sail off to and conquer and rule for well over two centuries now—they had been ruling it before even a single European colony was successfully set in the New World, first as the far-flung fiefdom of the Dutch East India trading company and then, since 1800, under the rule of the Dutch government itself. All for the love of cloves . . . and coffee, sugar, rice, tea, indigo, spices, gutta-percha, india rubber, tobacco, mother of pearl, tortoise shells, pearls, pepper, and palm oil.

By the 18th of September 1832, the *James Maury*'s cargo was secured in Batavia, her holds filled with Javanese coffee. Captain Woodbury awaited only an evening breeze and the ebb.

When Moses Grandy awakened belowdecks on the day they would sail, he heard music. Over his head he pulled on a cotton shirt, then climbed the short steep ladder and went above, following the muted tones, opened his eyes to a sultry, blue-sky morning, and peered over the rail. Fifty yards distant two Javanese women, one about thirty and the other half that age, sat on crates on the quay, and nestled between them lay a box that the younger one was playing with mallets, pouring forth the tune that pulled Grandy toward it.

Both of the women that he now approached wore sarongs, gaily patterned with long, thin white triangles, like sugarcane leaves, and fern fronds against a field of green or brown, and the older of the two, the one in brown, had a checked jacket about her shoulders. She had begun to sing along with the round-noted tune the younger one played on a xylophone of round teak bars, lightly hammering with two felt-tipped mallets that flexed and bent as her hands rose and fell. Moses stood as one enchanted, for, though he could not understand a word the Javanese woman sang, he could grasp the borderless, nationless inflections of yearning, as they could also grasp him.

The docks of Batavia were coming to life, though neither woman seemed to notice the high carts rolling past, nor the tall black man standing by them, though he knew they had marked his drawing near. He had sailed around Cape Horn, endured its wild storm-along winds and rains, and crossed thousands of miles of open ocean, just to be captivated, captured even, by this concert on the quay. In a few moments in a faraway port, the song of the two women had yanked him at once back to the slanted porch on his mother's cabin, where she so often sat and rocked, blind, infirm, robbed of her young, yet even in decline singing with dignity of thunder rolling and lightning flashing and children crying, their song pulling him back swiftly also to the dark juniper waters of the Pasquotank and Sawyer's ferry and plantation.

And, once there, to his wife.

How had they done this to him? How had these women who had never laid eyes upon him before this moment still somehow and with such ease laid him bare? Gone right past his seeing eyes and knowing mind and found here at the edge of the trackless seas the path to his very heart?

Suddenly the song ended. From his reverie and through his tears Moses Grandy saw the both of them now regarding him and smiling at him, the older one speaking frankly, asking of him, "Mister likes *gambang*?" as she tapped one of the teak bars lightly yet still with enough of a touch to make it sing a note.

"Yes," says Moses. "Yes, I like the *gambang*. And I like your song." Touching his lips.

She smiled more broadly now, and she raised her left hand slowly to her throat, showing him as she did a slender gold band on her fourth finger. Ah, she is married, he thought. She has a man.

"Is your man a sailor?" asked Moses Grandy, gesturing to the *James Maury* and the other ships along the quay. She followed his movement, but she did not answer, only smiled and hummed, as the younger woman flexed the mallets, mere splints of horn, and began another song. Now Moses was invisible to them again—he reached into his pocket and brought forth a large American copper penny, the only coin he had on him, and placed it in the older one's left hand, heard it clink against her ring, and then he turned to go back to his ship. The women were a little louder this time, and something more urgent, less mournful, found its way on the air from them to him.

Moses Grandy climbed the *James Maury*'s gangplank, day-dreaming of home, already there.

———

At the end of the *James Maury*'s Batavian voyage, with the three hundred dollars he had earned and by the good offices of Virginia intermediaries, his old merchant friends in Norfolk, Moses Grandy bid for and bought his second wife from Enoch Sawyer's heirs—the old man five years dead and in the Camden ground now. She journeyed to Boston, where she and Moses Grandy began to live together at long last, free.

> No more, boys, no more, go to sea no more.
> Get married instead and spend all night in bed and go to sea
> no more.

The Wind That Blows, 1830

David Walker's September 1829 *Appeal*, published in Boston, is a call to arms from one degraded black man—as he terms himself in print—to as many others as his pamphlet can reach, and it feeds the fear of slave uprisings and race war and stiffens many spines for what may come, and soon does. Whether he reads Walker or not, the smart, literate, "bright-skinned" slave Nat Turner has visions, sees blood on the leaves of corn in a field, and hears the word of God, he claims, word that he should to go forth in rebellion and kill white people. In August 1831 in Southampton County, Virginia, he does just that, leaving fifty-five whites dead and ensuring a violent reprisal that will see five times as many of his own people killed and repressive laws toward them passed all across the South.

Nor is a spirit of rebellion limited to people of color. The former vice president of the United States, South Carolinian John C. Calhoun, as staunch a believer in the Southern order of the day as walks the world, is fomenting an uprising in his native state, inventing a Nullifier Party, nodding to England and bowing to cotton and having his home state legislature nullify federal tariffs, "abominations" in the South Carolinians' sight and parlance. President Jackson achieves a Force Bill in Congress and, using its authority to enforce federal laws in the states, he sails ships of the U.S. Navy into Charleston Bay (no matter to him that South Carolina has also nullified the Force Bill). Henry Clay modifies a compromise tariff to suit Calhoun and matters do not come to blows in the Palmetto State.

And the fever cools again.

Though not in New England, home of the forceful, unyielding, unpopular abolitionists. Men stone the poet John Greenleaf Whittier and the English antislavery campaigner George Thompson. A mob breaks up a session of the female antislavery society and drags William Lloyd Garrison through the streets of Boston with a noose around his neck. Only the city's mayor and a protective night in what the *Hampshire Gazette* calls "the dank vapors of a dungeon" save him.

Grandy and Maffitt, Late 1834

North End and Charlestown Navy Yard
Boston, Massachusetts
LATE 1834

GRANDY

Just below the big, high, open burying ground of Copp's Hill runs Charter Street, where the free blacks live, below the graveyard and above the older New Guinea community down closer to the water. Moses Grandy lives here, too, walks the narrow North End lanes, takes time to himself amidst the graves and watches the work going on just across the Charles River at the Charlestown Navy Yard. Hears it, too, as the shipwrights and caulkers still pound away day after week after month on the USS *Constitution*, making it worthy again, getting it ready. Ready for what? Moses asks people around him. World tour, some say. Big world, he thinks, but that yonder's a big ship, too. He stands in the grass and weeds of Copp's Hill amidst the dull dark-gray slates, some standing straight, some leaning, knifed down and canted in the ground: dead men named Caleb and Benjamin, women named Dorcas and Mercy, so many of them sleeping unknowing beneath gravemarkers each with a skull and angel wings at its carved cap.

Late afternoon sometimes, coming home from the docks and wharves Moses Grandy stands in this small, high-up city of the dead and watches the living men swarming that craft over there. Boys, too, and that makes him smile. *Yeah, well—you got to learn ropes and riggings somehow, you boys, so go to it. I'd be a good man to have, on a ship like that. U.S. Navy. I reckon there ain't a man jack amongst 'em I couldn't tell him something about boats he don't know but needs to. . . .*

Copp's Hill Burying Ground, Boston

MAFFITT

And then one fall day the boys, the young acting midshipmen, get a closer look, just a glimpse, at the craft that will in the spring be their ship. Under a lieutenant's direction and watchful eye they walk solemnly but with discernible excitement toward the ship, and they try to maintain discipline and not clamber as they reach the gangplank. Now they are upon the spar deck, staring up at the masts fore, main, and mizzen, and the yards, the whole complex and spun world of hawsers and hemp rigging and belaying pins and tar. And now they go below, first to the gundeck, where the cannon in lines protrude through the hull and where the cook rules the forward domain, the great wooden "steep" barrel off to starboard where salt pork and salt beef soak their brine out in fresh water before the cook stews them, and the grog barrel where a mélange of rum and lemon and molasses and water keeps the crew going and unscurvied, the captain's cabin aft and its curved windows giving him a broad view off to the sides, and of where they will have been.

Then one more level below, to the berth deck, where they will live and carry on in the reefers' den at the central part of this deck, the officers sequestered in their wardroom aft filled with black tables and chairs, and the canvas hammocks hanging by ropes from iron hooks, cheek by jowl, the only daylight coming in through thin iron pipeshafts to porthole windows through the ship's two-foot live-oak hull.

Back up top they roam forward as one, the lieutenant climbing steep steps up the bowsprit toward a spar. They regard the long deck planks and the pegs holding them down, as the officer reminds them that there is no talk at all on deck and up in the rigging but talk of work and orders.

From this prospect John Maffitt looks back at Boston, hearing the bells tolling from the Old North Church high on Copp's Hill above the waters. Just off to the chapel's right he sees the old burying ground, too, where the man Hartt who built and launched this ship so many years ago lies buried. John Maffitt can make out people moving in the lanes across the river; and he can make out one lone, solitary figure up above it all in the naked graveyard.

Proud and secure of his future, young Maffitt stands on the spar deck of the USS *Constitution*, and this is his view of it, and out from it.

Maffitt, 1834–1842

Aboard the USS *Constitution*

1834–1835

Leaving Ellerslie and the South again, Acting Mid-shipman Maffitt next reported, on September 18, 1834, to the Boston Navy Yard, where the old frigate USS *Constitution* had been undergoing a lengthy, near-total restoration. The navy yard's commandant, who would become the commodore of the *Constitution* and appoint Maffitt his aide, was Captain Jesse D. Elliott—or Old Bruin, as Maffitt's fellow midshipmen had nicknamed him.

Maffitt quickly found that he had arrived in the port city amidst a row. Captain Elliott, an enthusiastic, bombastic man, had commissioned a carved wooden figurehead for the old ship and, instead of envisioning a mythical beast or a goddess, his choice to lead the *Constitution* into the foaming brine was a full-bodied likeness of the sitting President, Andrew Jackson of Tennessee. So incensed were the Whigs of Boston, so crosswise were they over Elliott's installation of such an obviously partisan work of art, that one of their number, a man named Dewey, muffled his oars and rowed out to the ship in a skiff one night and assaulted the wooden commander in chief, laid sawteeth to his chin and neck and carried the head away in a jute sack.

Young Maffitt, who took lessons ashore all fall and early winter at the navy yard (he marked well Steel's London cuartos, *The Elements and Practice of Rigging and Seamanship*), was ordered onto the ship itself on February 17, 1835, and, as he approached, saw just how Commodore Elliott had dealt with the headless President, by covering him with canvas. The dory that carried Maffitt from shore rowed up alongside the *Constitution*, lingering at the ladder only long enough to allow Midshipman Maffitt—now sporting long dark trousers flared at the bottom, a short jacket and vest over his shirt, and a black hat—to embark. He pulled himself up the side of the dark hull, climbed aboard, and presented himself to the officer of the deck, who sent him to the lieutenant with his orders.

"Who's aboard that I might know?" Maffitt asked the officer. Quite a few, it turned out, and presently he followed their laughter and their songs in steerage, found them in the reefer's den, heart and soul of midshipmen's life belowdecks.

One boy was strumming away on guitar, singing his fool head off—he knew everything, all the *haul-aways* and most of *Moore's Melodies*, and he did not stop so long as even one other still sang with him. When the reefers saw the new arrival and shouted, "Here's John Maffitt!" his young heart lifted and he joined them lustily in song:

> The minstrel boy to the war is gone
> In the ranks of death you'll find him.
> His father's sword he has girded on
> And his wild harp slung behind him.

Then someone worked that age-old magic with a corkscrew and a bottle of wine, and soon, though Maffitt had no girl he'd left behind, other than his sisterly cousin, Eliza, back at Ellerslie, he fell in just as passionately as anyone else with the great, noisy Saturday night toasts.

"Sweethearts and wives!"

"*Huzzah!*" And then they toasted again.

"The wind that blows—"

"*Huzzah!*"

"—and the ship that goes—"

"*Huzzah!*"

"—and the lass that loves a sailor!"

"*Huzzah, huzzah, huzzah!*"

Perhaps it is true, John Maffitt thought as they sing on into the night. Perhaps my bonnie does lie over the ocean! He would cross it, then, and find out. There could scarcely be a jollier lot, or a more enlivened crew than this one, to light out with. They were his brothers in arms, his comrades on the bounding main.

John Newland Maffitt, five days shy of sixteen, was off to see the wide world.

Before the *Constitution* left Boston harbor in March 1835 and sailed for New York, Commodore Elliott engaged another artist, a painter this time from his own naval ranks, to create upon the figurehead's protective canvas an American flag, one with an editorial message that could be seen and deciphered by any Whig observer with a glass who might be following the great ship's progress as she went down the Narrows Channel and threaded between Lovell's Island to starboard and the mile-long spit off Great Brewster to port. Something amiss with that flag, Commodore Elliott wished the Whigs to apprehend—the stripes for the New England states were nowhere to be seen! The captain's artist had omitted them under orders, Elliott's sign to the Bostonians that he considered the President's mutilation to have been the soul of disloyalty.

After provisioning in New York City, the USS *Constitution* on March 16, 1835, set off for Le Havre, France, there to collect American ambassador Edward Livingston, who had been invited to leave the country (a serious breach in U.S.-French diplomatic relations had occurred when France refused to pay American claims for ruined property dating back to Napoleon). On the voyage over, Commodore Elliott's ship and crew encountered an enormous equinoctial storm, a blow of such ferocity it washed a two-ton foc'sle cannon overboard, yet still tethered. The cannon slammed repeatedly into the hull's side, like a mad pendulum, till a fast-acting sailor chopped the line with an axe, losing the cannon but saving the great vessel from being gouged and sunk by its own weapon. Into Le Havre she sailed on the 10th of April 1835, and then, with Ambassador Livingston aboard, on to Plymouth, England, from which she headed back to New York on May 16, 1835.

Again heavy weather bedeviled the *Constitution*.

Is one great storm not enough? mused Maffitt. *Must we be spared by a late-winter nor'easter only to be shipwrecked now by a springtime English gale?*

Commodore Elliott mustered every seagoing talent he could bring to bear in threading the needle between ocean rocks and the waves breaking upon the Scilly Islands, pushing through at nine knots, mainmast twisting and groaning and a general fear among those aboard ship that she would be dismasted in the night and they would all be lost.

Yet they were not—Old Bruin kept up speed and brought them through and then cried out the general order, once all danger was past: "Splice the main brace!"

Everyone, including John Maffitt and his young comrades, gathered about the grog barrel, where it was rye for one and for rye all, and the *huzzah*s rang out, and a jolly lot they were again. This is adventure! This is the life, Maffitt reckoned, the one true life for me!

And the *Constitution* sailed back into New York harbor on June 22, 1835.

Piraeus, Greece

Down an ancient and crumbling road the midshipmen ran, thence to the Acropolis, to the Parthenon, and through the narrow, filthy streets of Athens, where the young men perceived the rude houses as having been built from pieces of storied ruins.

The next morning, John Maffitt, the commodore's aide in full brass-buttoned dress (gold braid, high collar, hat cocked), along with fifteen sailors at the oars, took the ship's barge to the Piraeus wharf and awaited the arrival of his charges—the king and queen of Greece, who were to visit and review and be feted shipboard. A troop of Bavarian cavalry soon cantered out upon the wharf, a carriage, too, and another troop. King Otho, resplendent in a Bavarian general's uniform and wearing the medal of St. Hubertus, lifted fifteen-year-old Queen Amalie down from the carriage, Maffitt escorted her to her seat in the aft of the barge, and the royal party was away. A breeze kicked up as the barge plied its way back to the *Constitution*, and spray flew from the oars toward those in the rear. Quickly Maffitt removed his blue cloak and wrapped it around the queen.

The *Constitution*'s officers were on the quarterdeck, the marine guards presented arms, and the ship's band played the national air, "Sons of Greece, Come, Arise." The royals and the admiral of the Greek navy inspected the great American ship slowly, carefully, and the Americans fired cannon for them, as both example and salute, and then performed one gymnastical show of boarding a ship in wartime and another of repelling boarders.

At dusk a sailor lit candles held aloft by the guards' rifles leaning in the spokes of the capstan, a nautical candelabrum. Queen Amalie, wishing to waltz, cajoled the ready band, and melodies in three-quarter time came cascading over the frigate's decks and out over the waters of the Mirtoon Sea, and Otho and Amalie spun together and she—in tasseled red hat and crimson coat, white dress, and red velvet leggings—seemed to all a pure dream, a light blue silk scarf around her waist floating in the sea air as she turned gaily to the tunes. She sent a young man from her entourage to Commodore Elliott, begging for a dance from the old sailor, but he demurred.

"My aide," said the commodore, "stands in for me in all such affairs."

Before Midshipman Maffitt could have a moment's thought, she was spinning him with her around the deck, he the boy from Ellerslie on Blount's Creek, North Carolina, who only yesterday trod the Acropolis and stood upon Mars Hill. Later, after the *Constitution*'s twenty-one-gun salute, when he floated the barge and the guests back to land at two in the morning, he would again drape his cloak about Amalie, and she would respond by inviting him to a ball at the palace. Such a night: Maffitt scarcely eighteen years old, and here he was upon the deck of a great American warship, out on the wine-dark sea of Odysseus, waltzing with the one and only queen of Greece in his arms.

Such a night.

Port Mahon, Menorca

Mediterranean Sea

CIRCA 1837

Six midshipmen rose early this morning and found a heavy mist lying upon the harbor of Port Mahon. Quietly they stole through the town and made their way up the hillside to a grave-yard. It was not yet first light.

An insult between two proud Virginians, one having struck the other in a rage, the stricken one's honor offended, had brought them, compelled them even, to this. And all because John Maffitt had loaned his blue cloak to the one who became enraged when the other took it off the bedstead of the first and wore it out on deck and there left it in a wet, bedraggled heap—and then would not own up to it till yet another of the boys called him out.

So the boys now came to the graveyard at dawn to fight a duel.

Maffitt served as a second for the one to whom he loaned his cloak, and while there was still time he spoke coolly, clearly to both of them, begging them to reconcile and not to carry this through. Steadily a morning redness was coming on, filling the eastern sky—these were all sailors, and the message was well known to them all. In just a few moments, morning light would play across the hillside and the graveyard's crooked crosses, its barren thorns.

The boy who took the blow was defiant, and he would not back down.

Now a latch was thrown, a dark velvet-lined box noiselessly opened. The principals looked briefly at the two blued percussion pistols, .45 caliber, with ten-inch barrels and burled walnut grips with silver inlay, made by an artist in Philadelphia with this very morning in mind.

One for each young man.

In a foreign field, on a lane that ran by the recent and the long dead, the two parties separated and positioned themselves twenty paces from each other. One last entreaty from John Maffitt. One last rebuff. The seconds moved off to the side. Maffitt did the counting, and on his "Three!" the duelists fired.

Neither moved for a moment, till the offended boy tottered, crumpled as he dropped to the ground, bleeding into the dust from the wound in his chest. He lay there muttering as his life flowed from him, speaking so softly that his comrades, trying to stanch the bleeding, must lean in to catch his dying words: "Mother . . . Emily . . . I love you. . . ." Crying out more loudly was the other, the more accurate shot of the two: "You must live—you must live else I am a wretch forever!"

John Maffitt rued the breaking of this day—they all did. The blood-red morning sun now sat easily upon the horizon away to the east and lacquered the dark Mediterranean Sea, with crimson gold, high-piled cumulus clouds holding the sun like a gift on this, as lovely a morning as the Balearic Islands ever saw.

Yet in full gloom the young seamen marched slowly, ferrying their comrade's body back to the ship, and heavy in their hearts, a tragedy on their hands.

Sailors, take warning.

Valleta, Malta

FEBRUARY 22, 1838

Early in the morning of February 22, 1838, the USS *Constitution* swung easy on her chains at anchor in the harbor at Valleta, Malta, as John Maffitt and his fellows helped decorate the ship to celebrate George Washington's birthday. The late Revolutionary general and first President was born on this day in 1732, and the boys made much of the 106-year-old man as they hung flags and pennants all about the ship's rigging.

By the time the *Constitution* was dressed, she flew nearly sixty flags and pennants, the American stars and stripes on foremast and mizzen and also as her ensign, a dark blue burgee atop the main. Other ships of the Mediterranean Squadron sported the colors, but none had the outpouring of decor of the *Constitution*, which regularly during the day fired cannonades and sent thunderclaps throughout the harbor, pounding off the great tawny walls of Fort St. Elmo. Gondolas with gay red-and-white and blue-and-white rounded tenting moved about the water, and ten British sailors on a ship's longboat stood and raised their oars in unison in tribute to Washington and to the heavens that held him. Everywhere around the harbor men and women gathered, cheering.

Maffitt and the boys kept it up till they were all about to drop. Tomorrow, quietly, they would strike the pennantry and fold the flags and put them away till the next great occasion, but just now

USS Constitution *in Malta on Washington's Birthday, February 22, 1838*

they were joining in to the full measure of their spirits and were all about revelry. John Maffitt waved his low-crowned black hat with the rest, as if he were saluting someone in particular across the way, as if he could see through all the cannon smoke the artist James Evans, who was set up with a field easel over there near the fort, getting it all down, painting away.

The midshipman was full-hearted, very stirred, for this was his birthday, too.

Today John Newland Maffitt turned nineteen.

Aboard the USS *Shark*

MARCH 1838

In the vast North Atlantic Ocean, halfway between the she-bangs of seaside Europe and the grogshops of Norfolk, Virginia, the men of the *Shark* were thirsty. Their leaders saw no one on deck except a lone midshipman, and, though he was on occasion the officer of the deck, he was not of the ship's regular command; he was only finding passage back to the United States with her.

A metal bar and a mallet were all they needed, and then, with main strength and ignorance, the lock and clasp came flying off the ship's spirit-room door. Rum and rye flowed quickly, and the crew was quickly getting good and drunk, the sailors spreading out along the rails. Their plot may have been hatched in secrecy, but now they had no cares, and their bravado and boisterous singing gave them all away:

> When I first came to Caroline, got drunk as drunk could be.
> I drank it neat, it was a treat to see what gals could be.
> Me heart is not me own, my boys, as I looks back to shore.
> A man must be blind to make up his mind to go to sea once
> more.

An officer appeared, Lieutenant Maxwell Woodhull, who judged the *Shark* "in possession of the crew." Mutinously they sang and swayed, and as always there were far more sailors than officers aboard ship.

Before Woodhull could act, Midshipman Maffitt ran forward and went forcefully among the men, ordering them to quarters, cajoling them, laughing if he must, singing with them, too, but also beseeching them—"Who has done this? Who started this?" He helped Woodhull and, now, several other officers round up the three men who had engendered the affair and cart them off to the ship's brig.

"Who are you, sir?" one officer asked the young man.

"Acting Midshipman Maffitt, sir. I was Commodore Elliott's aide on the *Constitution*."

"Well done," the officer replied. "And duly noted."

After twenty-nine days at sea, the *Shark* tied up at sheer's wharf, Gosport Navy Yard, Norfolk, Virginia, and what might have been a successful mutiny and a disaster at sea was now down in her log only as an unfortunate incident. The main credit for quelling it, for shutting it down and collaring its instigators went to young Maffitt. Ashore in Norfolk, he was toasted aplenty, and his shipmates sent the extra oysters at the table down his way, and his way only.

Aboard the *Woodbury, Vandalia,* and *Macedonian*
Pensacola, Florida, and Gulf Squadron
1838–1842

In Washington, D.C., that June, John Maffitt faced seven examiners in the Exchange Hotel—five stern, senior Navy men and two professors, who turned and sifted and grilled him to their satisfaction. He knew how to bend a sail to its yard. He knew how to stow the hold, how to station officers and crew. He knew all manner of navigation from the incomparable cipherings of Bowditch, and of knottings and splicings of ropes, lines, hawsers, and cables, and of rigging from Steel. He knew gunnery. He knew how to tend ship at a single anchor, and he especially knew when asked how to hoist a frigate's boats in tow in a rising wind (which examiner Isaac Hull had done with the *Constitution* while five British ships gave chase back in the War of 1812, a tale the young man had heard and, all to the good, remembered). He knew his stuff all right, and he left the Exchange a passed midshipman.

Afterward, John Maffitt served first on the packet *Woodbury*, which patrolled the Gulf of Mexico looking for Mexican privateers and then lay to for repairs in the port of Vera Cruz, Mexico, also bearing witness while the French—at war with Mexico—bombarded the place. Transferred to the sloop of war *Vandalia*, stationed at Pensacola Navy Yard, he sailed with her in early 1839, when the *Vandalia* was blasted and buffeted by heavy weather before she reached Vera Cruz and the aftermath of the French martial storm.

Maffitt gazed upon the French fleet, now at anchor, that had taken the city and the castle of San Juan de Ulúa. Twenty years old and a lieutenant now (having been given the rank after one of the gales tossed the ship's previous officer overboard), he went ashore and wandered Vera Cruz by himself, thinking himself a second Don Quixote, striding alone in street and alley seeking as always adventure, levity, company. He looked to the balconies of the city's

Alameda, expecting that on one of them a young woman might appear, curious, becoming, enchanting, hastened to her balcony by the sound of his approach.

But the city was totally deserted and he was utterly alone.

The French bombardment had torn this place apart with shot and shell, pocked the walls everywhere, driven all the people out of Vera Cruz, and Lieutenant Maffitt came across no one, heard nothing but his very own footsteps ringing on the flagstones.

Later that spring, Lieutenant Maffitt went out and sounded the channel where the Rio Grande came down to the gulf. In the *Vandalia*'s ship's boat he was storm tossed, driven ashore, and, before completing his assignment, he wound up spending two days in the hovels of poor fishermen on a sandbar island they called Bagdad. He would come to know the coast of Mexico ever better—in May a year later he sailed on the *Macedonian* from Pensacola to Campeche, from Campeche on to Vera Cruz, where he wrote his cousin in June 1840, then on to Tampico before heading back to Florida just in time for hurricane season, August and September. Lieutenant Maffitt was detached for three months' leave on October 22, 1840, and there he was in the gorgeous Florida autumn.

Only a day's ride by horse or carriage through the panhandle's longleaf pine barrens stood between Mobile, Alabama, and Pensacola, and the long white-sand beaches of the Florida barrier islands drew society folks down from Mobile Bay to this town on the gulf with its deep water and sea breezes, its palmettos and tall ships and young officers. When the Alabama beauty Mary Florence Murrell of the Mobile Murrells came to visit kin in Pensacola during October 1840, there she met the twenty-one-year-old Acting Lieutenant John N. Maffitt, now attached to a great prize of the War of 1812, the frigate USS *Macedonian*.

"Pensacola," he had once thought and written to his cousin, "is dull and uninteresting, very few ladies who are desirable associates." But that was an utterance he had made over a year and a half before, and now his heart and mind were changed.

The winds of romance whirled, and rapidly so. Having known each other scarcely a month, Mary Murrell and John Maffitt were married in Mobile on November 17, 1840. By the end of the next October, Maffitt was the *Macedonian*'s acting master. When their first child—a girl—was born in February 1842, he was at sea. But his ship would soon touch again at Pensacola and, when it did, their daughter would be baptized shipboard by the *Macedonian*'s chaplain: Mary Florence Maffitt.

They would call her Florie.

Grandy, Mid-1830s–1842

American East Coast

MID-1830S

From the wharf at Norfolk, men watched the tall black man standing at the ship's rail. Though it had been quite some years now, many of them still recognized Moses Grandy from his freightboating days, when he was well known among them, and they called up to him in warning: "Stay aboard. It is now against the law for you to disembark and walk the land. Do not risk arrest by stepping onto Virginia soil."

The town's mayor, out walking the docks, saw him, too—"You've been too long amongst the Yankees, Moses," said His Honor—and ordered him to leave Norfolk before nine days were passed.

"If you are not gone by then," the mayor said, "I will sell you for the good of the state of Virginia."

Moses Grandy had journeyed here to buy the freedom of his fifteen-year-old son, whose master had written to Grandy in Boston and agreed to sell the boy to his father for three hundred dollars. Yet now, when Moses Grandy appeared in Norfolk and presented the owner with that sum, the man refused it.

The price had gone up, his boy's master said, to $450.

Way short of that, and thus denied and empty-handed, Moses Grandy returned swiftly to his ship and waited.

Two vessels sailing over from the Eastern shore filled with Negroes and cattle came into Norfolk's harbor, and Grandy listened to the paired sounds of cattle lowing and slaves wailing in despair, dreadful music, an awful chorus of lament. A white man with a whip worked on board each vessel to keep them quiet, and the ships neared and then lay by his own. All the horrors of Moses Grandy's Carolina past suddenly reared up, engulfing him in terror. *Before I would be a slave again!* he thought, apprehensive about everything around him. At one point the approach of men by boat—he took them for policemen sent by the mayor to seize and imprison him—forced him to the edge of fatal action. His hands on his ship's rough rail, sticky with sea salt, he stared overboard in full-fledged alarm.

Twice Moses Grandy nearly leapt overboard into the waters of Hampton Roads to be carried off by the swift-running, ocean-bound tide, to drown himself in the ebb. But each time some inward power, some strength and presence of mind kept him from it: *I have come too far, at too much cost, lost too much, time, company, love. Can't stop now, can't stop now. Don't jump, Moses, come what may now, don't jump.*

Directly his ship weighed anchor and left Hampton Roads, northbound for New York City. Nor'easterlies slowed and stalled the ship, which then turned into Delaware Bay and stood for a sheltered anchorage twenty-five miles north of Cape May, just inside the mouth of Maurice's River, New Jersey, to lay up there till the headwinds abated. Moses Grandy, still in a state, felt he had had such a close call with reenslavement that he dared not make a return trip from New York to Norfolk. In an abject fever to get off the ship as soon as it anchored, he begged his captain to put him ashore near the fishing villages of Bivalve and Port Norris, and the captain at last granted him his wish.

"When I once more touched the free land," Moses would later recall, "the burthen of my mind was removed: if a two-ton weight had been taken off me, the relief would not have seemed so great."

For two days Moses Grandy struggled to make it to Philadelphia, covering fifty miles on foot and by wagon, and once there, where years before he had worked for some months and where he still had friends, he dictated a letter and had it sent to his wife in Boston to let her know that he was safe and on his way home. Once back in Boston, he borrowed $160 and added it to the $300 he already had. Then he turned right around and traveled back down to New York City, where a friend, one John Williams, saw to it that Grandy's $450 would safely reach Norfolk and satisfy the owner of his son.

"Thus," Moses Grandy would later say, "I bought my son's freedom. I met him at New York, and brought him on to Boston."

Boston, Massachusetts

In 1836 Moses Grandy and his wife and son were living on Copp's Hill, the highest spot in Boston's North End, among the free blacks of Charter Street. The street ran right past the old Copp's Hill cemetery, where many of their kinsmen and women were now buried near Cotton Mather, who hunted witches in Salem, and shipwright Edmund Hartt, who built the USS *Constitution*, and so many others of Boston's revered dead.

What a time to be alive and here in this place! Moses Grandy thought, as he strode between his home and the docks. Once he nearly stumbled into a small parade—the Boston Brigade Band, marching ahead of the Boston Light Infantry and playing a sharp, brassy tune in honor of the infantry's anniversary, "The Tiger Quick Step." Another day he was startled by Charles F. Durant, the sky-invader who had amazed a sell-out crowd at the stadium by inflating a balloon with hot air and then drifting above Boston at an elevation of 150 feet, tipping his top hat to those below. *Well, Grandy mused, not everybody has himself a balloon, but if you got a high spot like Copp's Hill you can sure enough see a ways, see the Old North Church here, see way out the harbor and all the rocky islands, see on over the river Charles, see Charlestown, the navy yard, all of it.*

When spring returned to Boston in late May 1836, so, too, did the New England abolitionists, coming back for another convention, their third, from all across the northeast, and when Moses Grandy got word of this he figured he would once again be there among them. They went into session on Tuesday, May 22, and Grandy came early to the hall and stayed late. During the afternoon session, Mister Henry Stanton spoke up, declaring there was at this very moment "a colored man now in this house, who has paid eighteen hundred dollars, the earning of his own hands, to buy his own body, and purchase his wife out of slavery. His children have been sold he knows not where. This shows what the slave will do to get his freedoms!"

Murmurs and gasps sounded in the crowd, five hundred strong, and then came the cries.

"Where is he?"

"Let's see him!"

"Bring him forth!"

Till the tall man himself walked forward boldly and took his place upon the dais and told the tale in his own words: "My name is Moses Grandy. I was once a slave in North Carolina. My master said he gave me a chance to buy myself. I worked nights for it—tended corn and got out staves in the woods. Well, I gived him six hundred dollars for to buy myself, and he turns round and sells me to another man. I was an orphan when he sold me. I paid him the money, little by little, when I earn it. Well, I turned round and told my new master, who didn't know I had bought myself, and he said I might again. So I went to work in a canal boat, had a good chance, and bought myself again, but just then, my master got into difficulty: his estate was sold and I along with it. I got a good master that time, and he let me buy my liberty, and put the money I earn into another man's hands. When I earn enough, he sent me to Providence, and make a free man of me. I bought my wife for three hundred dollars. My children were sold and carried off, and I can't tell where they are."

A man standing close by, incredulous at Moses Grandy's report, challenged him sharply at once: "Why, they say a Negro is incapable of taking care of himself. How could this man pay for himself three times?"

Again murmurs and muttering suffused the air—perhaps the man was right, perhaps Grandy was a teller of tales. Anyone could say anything he wanted to, after all. This was a country filled with straightfaced frauds who lied to gain attention, favor, office, and profit. How did they know what this Grandy said was true?

"Look there," said Grandy, furiously thrusting forth his two bulky arms, showing his muscles and balling his fists. "These arms could work for my masters all day, and earn enough in nights to buy myself three times—and they did!"

Mister Stanton tried to settle the mixed tempers of the crowd, saying: "It is not uncommon for slaves to earn themselves by extra labor, and then they are afterwards sold again." A Virginian named Taylor said, "I know a case of a person in Norfolk, who had permitted a slave to buy himself, and when he had earned two thirds of the price, his master sold him. Give a Negro the motive of liberty, and he will do the work of three slaves."

Everyone seemed fatigued from travel and from the long opening day, and there were three more days of this yet to come, so at six o'clock the convention adjourned till the next morning. Moses Grandy glared at the man who had made such noisy misgivings about his story of life back in Carolina. He wanted to grip the man hard and shake sense into him, but he restrained himself and instead shook hands with Mister Stanton, then left the hall as directly as he could, down an aisle full of folks who also wanted to take his hand, feel his grip, squeeze his shoulder, and wish him well.

Even so, Moses would not be back in the morning.

He had to work.

———

All through the 1830s Moses Grandy was a familiar figure around Boston, the tall, strong, plainspoken man of the docks, the ardent abolitionist, ten years or and more a strider of the old port's streets and hills. The presence in Boston of his wife and his son pleased him immensely, yet their very nearness made him look afar and want more—his sister Tamar back in Elizabeth City in North Carolina, his children who had been sold off in New Orleans—he yearned to make enough money, somehow, and buy them all, just as he had bought himself and his wife and his son. And his brother, too, the one they kidnapped away right when he had come back to Elizabeth City from the West Indies, thrown him down on a loose door and shackled him right to it, carrying him off like a man on a cooling board.

But Moses Grandy was nearly twenty years older now (about fifty, he guessed) than when he had worked to buy himself three times down in Carolina. How could there possibly be enough hours in the day and night, enough years left, for him to accomplish and earn all he needed? How much time would he have to spend away from wife and family? Was he cheating those he loved and had right here? Yet he continued undeterred. He could remember men, friends of his, working in water, before dawn till after dusk, chopping with picks and shovels or pulling with their bare worn and torn hands at roots under the dark water, roots they could see, cutting the ditches and canals around the great swamps, and he remembered well how, if they could but keep their heads above the water, they worked on. If those men could keep on, he could, too, and he would. He would sleep, but he would not rest or know peace of heart until he had found and bought back as many of his kin as he could. That was the way of the world for him, the way he knew it to work, and his lot was to fulfill the promise that had started with his own triumph, or to die trying.

By 1840, the Grandys were living at 223 Ann Street in Boston's Second Ward, a rough waterside world of sailors at liberty and drafty taverns with fiddles squawling and brothels, too, bounded by Hanover and Cross Streets on down to Commercial Street and the harbor: from Granite Wharf to Lewis Wharf and the East Boston Ferry, on up to Union Wharf and the marine railways, and Battery Wharf and the Winnisimett Ferry beyond. The New Market was Grandy's market, and the Second Ward streets were full early to late clattering with four-in-hands of every sort, from fine black carriages with gold and red trim to the draymen's wagons, with canvas over half-round metal hoops, drawn through the town by tawny Belgian drafthorses whose hooves rang out and whose pungent dung covered the cobblestones.

But soon thereafter Moses Grandy made a huge change.

After all this time in Massachusetts, Grandy moved his family—six of them now living under his roof, three young men below the age of twenty-three, one between twenty-four and thirty-five, as well as Moses and his wife—from Boston to Portland in the fall of 1841. Perhaps life would be more peaceable for free people of color a little farther up the New England coast.

Perhaps.

Four hundred free black people were now living and working in Portland, dozens of them as mariners, many of them worshipping at the Abyssinian Meeting House on Newbury Street, Munjoy Hill, right near the docks. Of late the Reverend Amos Noah Freeman had come to lead them, and in secrecy he used the meetinghouse to receive and hide escaped slaves from the South, and from there send them forth into freedom. Canada was not so far away.

Moses Grandy moved to Portland and he met Reverend Freeman. He met Nathan Winslow; he met (if he did not already know him from his visits to Boston) Reuben Ruby, the free black man with the horse-drawn hack, one of the abolitionist leaders of Maine and of all New England. He met the Reverend Samuel Clement Fessenden and his father, General Samuel Fessenden, a staunch abolitionist whose belief in African colonization as the solution to Negro slavery had been changed by hearing Garrison speak ten years earlier. These were Moses Grandy's people—he went among them, worked and worshipped with them, was one with and of them.

In this city in 1842 Reverend Fessenden, who came of age in a home where his father always welcomed runaways, chaired the first meeting of the Portland Union Antislavery Society.

Moses Grandy, sailor, captain, abolitionist, bore witness to its birth.

The Wind That Blows, 1840

In late August 1839, the brig USS *Washington* captures the schooner *Amistad* off Long Island, full of enslaved Africans who have mutinied and for nearly two months have been sailing the craft east and north to the United States, and Captain Richard Meade brings *Amistad* into the port of New London. For a year and a half the case of the *Amistad* and her mutinous slaves winds through American courts of law and public opinion, involving at times Senator John C. Calhoun of South Carolina, New York abolitionist Lewis Tappan, the minister from Spain, and former President John Quincy Adams. Adams argues for the *Amistad*'s mutineers before the U.S. Supreme Court, which affirms the lower courts and frees the Africans, ordering them returned to their native land, Sierra Leone, which they reach in January 1842.

At this time New Orleans, the Creole kingdom, the third-largest city in America, boasts the biggest slave market on the continent, Lamarque's slave pen on Common Street, Foster's on Baronne Street, and so many more. Auctioneers shout out prices for black men and women on the block, crying out over eager crowds in back-and-forth French and English, "Trois, three, trois et demi, three and a half, quatre, four, quatre et demi, four and a half, cinq, five!" Steamboats deliver slaves to market, horse-drawn carts draw them there, and more still come trooping in on foot, chained together by iron coffles.

The new nation keeps moving to the west, and new American territories below 36 degrees 30 minutes north longitude allow Negro slavery. Senator Calhoun looks out over all human history and, judging that life was ever thus, pronounces slavery "a positive good." Senator Thomas Hart Benton of Missouri (and also of North Carolina, where he was born in Hillsboro and briefly educated at the University of North Carolina in Chapel Hill, which expelled him for possession of a pistol on campus, or for the theft of the community's only gold dollar in his dormitory, whichever account one believes), slaveholder and author of the frankly villainous doctrine of "manifest destiny," hates Calhoun, opposes slavery for Texas, and ultimately declares himself to be "against the institution."

One Independence Day, a Massachusetts man moves into a cabin on a pond outside Concord; he is Henry Thoreau, an unknown writer there to draft the story of two weeks he and his late brother spent boating on the Concord and Merrimack Rivers some years before. Not too far away, in Boston, Garrison, one of the best-known authors in the nation, and in the South the most hated, continues to publish his abolitionist newspaper, *The Liberator*, never missing a single issue, unswerving in its calls for the immediate emancipation of all slaves everywhere in the United States of America.

Maffitt,
Early 1840s – Early 1850s

Washington, D.C.

EARLY 1840S

Lieutenant Maffitt climbed the marble steps of a church in the capital to hear the famous itinerant evangelical preacher hold forth. He was pressed and jostled before he even reached the huge wooden doors, and so crowded was the place that the preacher would have to enter it through a window and be passed hand over hand above the throng toward the pulpit. There was nothing new or unusual about this: this preacher had proselytized to packed churches and halls in Louisville, Cincinnati, Boston (filling a house there on only a few hours' notice), and New York, where he clambered up a ladder on the church's rear exterior wall and then descended to the pulpit through a portal above.

The wondrous preacher so many had come to hear and idolize was John Maffitt's father: Reverend John Newland Maffitt, whom the public prints called the Exile from Erin, the Prince of the Pulpit, the Methodist Meteor.

Presidents knew and admired him: he was a friend of Andrew Jackson, Old Hickory himself, and he converted Tippecanoe, President William Henry Harrison, who nonetheless succumbed to pneumonia thirty-two days after giving his inaugural address in the killing rain of a Washington winter's day. On December 6, 1841, Reverend Maffit would be made chaplain of the U.S. House of Representatives.

The young lieutenant marveled at the magnificent orator, whom he scarcely knew, though he knew much of him. He knew of the pair of gamblers who had entered a full assembly hall out West, one of them drawing a pistol that he cocked and fired, intending to blow a hole through the preacher's head. Instead, the bullet only lanced a curl from above Maffitt's ear, and the reverend neither flinched nor slowed his Shakespearean delivery. The gamblers, believing their aim to have been altered by divine intervention, ran forward and prostrated themselves before the preacher, following him on tour thereafter as his most eager acolytes and apostles.

Reverend Maffitt always fortified himself with a raw egg in a big snifter of brandy before he took the stage, and when he spoke of the Bible and demons always lurking and better days yet to come and redemption in the blood of the Lamb, in the grace of the Christ, and sin everywhere whether one could see it or not, all his listeners swooned.

Almost all.

If the Navy lieutenant sensed something histrionic, imprecise, even inauthentic about his father's theatricality, he did not admit it to himself. He had memorized the poem eulogizing his sister that the reverend penned a decade earlier, transcending grief for a few moments to do so—nothing but sincerity there. And here today, why, there was nothing false at all about the enthrallment in which the reverend held these hundreds, about their mesmerization, their enchantment. Lieutenant Maffitt knew well by now the power of the sea, of wind and wave, and were there not waves of feeling here in this room, swells of emotion bonding all these men and women, especially the women, who lunged forward to heap their jewelry—rings, brooches, necklaces, all—into the collection plates when Reverend Maffitt declared that the good work needed their help?

Yet the plates passed John Maffitt without gain. The lieutenant knew that he owed this man his life, everything, yet he also knew that, abandoned by him at five years of age, he also owed the preacher nothing at all. Nothing but a prayer: "Our Father, who art in Heaven, hallowed be thy name. . . ."

New England Waters

EARLY 1840S

By the end of 1842, Lieutenant Maffitt found himself surprised and pleased to be assigned to the U.S. Coast Survey, engendered thirty-five years earlier by the now aged German professor F. R. Hassler, to give President Jefferson what the nation needed: good, accurate charts of the coastlines, the shape of the harbor bottoms and the ocean floor at the inlet bars, of the shoals and rocks in the shipping lanes, and approaches to avoid them. Soon after Maffitt's joining the survey, Professor Hassler died, and a new director took over. Alexander Bache, great-grandson of Benjamin Franklin, kept John Maffitt on.

The Coast Survey was going to chart New England, and Superintendent Bache wanted the excellent young navigator and cartographer with him. So Maffitt moved his young family to Baltimore, where his and Mary Florence's second child, the boy Eugene Alexander, was born, and where Maffitt hired an old family friend—a trustworthy Irishman—to watch over his wife and children and take care of things regarding his family while he was gone.

And then the lieutenant was away to the Yankee coast.

Absence, folks said, makes the heart grow fonder—but of whom? An amatory affair occurred between Mary Florence Murrell Maffitt and another man not long after the lieutenant had shipped out. Maffitt was betrayed, he learned, and his family dissolved. With whom had his wife taken up? And why had she thrown him over? She had met him as a sailor, as an officer and a gentleman in a port town. She knew his career meant he would be gone for weeks and months on end. She knew he was a mariner. She knew . . .

Surely there were things behind the flash of her Alabama eyes he wished he might have seen and known, too. Rocks and emotional shoals invisible to his naked eye, unplumbed depths of spirit, the hidden dangers of an inconstant heart and mind that could tear the very keel out of a man's soul. Now that she had failed him, he would have Florie and Eugene sent to Ellerslie in Carolina, and the devil with Mary Murrell, of whom he would never speak again—he would drown all memory of her, not in strong drink as so many men in similar straits might do, but in the ocean itself. He was a son of Neptune, after all, and from the god of the sea, the earthshaker, he would draw his strength and sail on.

John Maffitt, a compact, energetic man with a small mouth, his dark eyes always steady and focused, now drove and threw himself headlong into shipboard life and into the work of the Coast Survey. If the sea and the edge of the sea could be read, he would be one of its prime readers. He would find lines and angles and messages from the shallows and the deep alike and then record and report them, an art for not its sake alone but the good of all those who go down to the sea in great ships and have business there. For all that was known, far more was unknown, and he, no underling beneath the stars, would reckon with both, bringing the former to bear on the latter, as he had since he first went off to school, stagecoach ticket on his lapel, and picked up his first compass and protractor and began to see the world as a sailor's sailor must.

Though the world may be described in so many ways—in a painting, a verse, or a song, even in the simple regard of birds, a count and report of Canada geese and their fellow flyers, swans down from the tundra, or of flights of cormorants along the rolling troughs of the sea close inshore—still and all, with all its numbers and its names, what a thing of beauty was a nautical chart. Oh, the names: the inlets, the thoroughfares and haulovers; the islands, spits and bights and channels; the rocks (call them Hens and Chickens as they did in Long Island Sound, or Indians as they did in the Sir Francis Drake Channel in the Virgin Islands, they were all still rocks); the soundings, the numbers, depths right down to where the weights hit, and on sand or mud or hard bottom; and the very ends of land, a point of marsh, a point of grass.

What a beauty was a chart.

Lieutenant Maffitt and his party aboard the schooner *Gallatin* would spend five years taking the measure of the northeast coast (the *Gallatin* was a 112-ton, 73-foot ship that had been among those sent into Charleston, South Carolina, to suppress nullification back in 1832). In 1845 he worked in and around New London, watching and recording the set and velocity and drift of the tides in Fisher's Island Sound, crafting a chart of his observations of currents that, in turn (in Bache's words), would make "practical deductions" from them "comparatively easy." In 1846 Maffitt's party discovered a massive, theretofore unknown shoal six miles south of Nantucket's South Shoal, an east-west shoal with only eight feet of water over it in places. In their work they were impeded by the elements, by storms, by fogs enveloping the shrouds so completely that ships working two miles apart could not see each other for days, by fire (Nantucket village burned on July 13 and 14 of that year). Yet they were trying to establish and state for mariners the world over how the old and new south shoals below Nantucket lay in relation each to each, and they worked on.

In 1847 Maffitt and his fellows were in Boston harbor, sounding Vineyard Sound, ciphering the hydrography of Hyannis harbor. By 1848 Maffitt was commanding the *Gallatin*, studying Muskeget Channel between Martha's Vineyard and Nantucket (the treacherous, fish-rich lane, its depths from forty to ninety feet, though shoals between the channel and Chappaquiddick carried less than ten feet), discovering new shoals, surviving a nor'easter, a heavy and damaging gale, when the *Gallatin* from off the Scituate rocks was standing for Boston harbor. After the repairs to her spars and sails, she worked on there, Maffitt observing the currents in the great harbor. In 1849 he took command for a spell of the schooner *Morris* and worked in Martha's Vineyard Sound. He sited a new lighthouse for New Bedford on Palmer's Island, and then he sailed the *Gallatin* on down the coast, into Delaware Bay and up the river that fed it, to the yards at Wilmington, where the *Gallatin* would undergo further repair and then ere long go into service graphing another great American harbor, Charleston, where, as the proud provincials would gladly tell him, the Ashley and the Cooper Rivers met to form the Atlantic Ocean.

Cape Hatteras, North Carolina

1850

Maffitt then appeared in the Graveyard of the Atlantic, sailed to Cape Hatteras. The sand spit at Cape Point had been growing for several years (ever since the great hurricane of September 1846 that opened both Hatteras Inlet to the southwest and Oregon Inlet to the north), advancing to the southwest nearly three-eighths of a mile. Lieutenant Maffitt's reconnaissance held that the Hatteras Island cove just to the north and west of Cape Point now made for a good harbor of refuge.

There the beach curved nicely and vessels anchored in the cove might sit snug in the cape's lee, and in four or five fathoms of water, their anchors resting on a bottom of soft blue mud. When the nor'easters blew twenty-five to thirty out over the shoals, the water in Hatteras Cove would be flat calm. Coming into this anchorage, mariners said, one moment you would be on your ear, the next you would be becalmed.

Maffitt had an eye out for harbors of refuge, and he had a knack for finding them—he also had his mind set just now on another one near Cape Romain, on down the shoreline in South Carolina. He read the coast like most men read newspapers, and he it was, he felt, who found the richer goods.

Beaufort, North Carolina

LATE 1850, EARLY 1851

The work of the Coast Survey went on unceasingly. In Beaufort harbor alone, the party with Lieutenant Maffitt commanding covered 53 miles with 1,289 soundings, measuring 88 angles and pulling up 36 samples from the bottom.

The zeal with which his men went after knowledge of the shores and the bottoms matched the effectiveness, and efficiency, with which they found it. They were mapping waterfront like no one ever had before, in Charleston finding a new entry for ships from the north and east, the Sullivan's Island Channel, and in North Carolina announcing publicly to the navigators of the world that there was a harbor of refuge to be found at Hatteras Cove, northwest of the cape's point and the dreaded Diamond Shoals. Between Charleston and Georgetown, they planned the harbor inside Bull's Bay, to be aided by a lighthouse Maffitt proposed for the northeast end of Bull's Island (a diked island home to a rice plantation and to black squirrels that ran all up and down its gigantic pines), where a bleached boneyard of skeletal pines and live oaks all fallen and thrashed together by wind and tides looked as if it had been woven that way by knowing hands.

Of a day, at rest and anchor in Beaufort harbor, from the *Gal-*

latin's quarterdeck Maffitt could well observe the fish houses and net shacks along Taylor's Creek in Beaufort, the old frame homes fronting the creek and harbor, many with balustrades, widow's walks, atop them. When he took the ship's boat into town and walked the port-town streets, he strode beneath pecan trees and elms, their leaves filtering and feathering the damp coastal light. Away from the water, beside the Purvis Chapel Methodist Episcopal Church (its low spire housing a church bell come all the way from Glasgow, Scotland), by shank's mare Maffitt had made his way to the town's old burying ground with its thin headstones and shafts, its live oaks and their broad, tangled evergreen crowns.

And now Lieutenant Maffitt stood at an old sailor's grave, lingered a moment, and mused upon that man and his life and times. At the western edge of the cemetery, just a few feet from Craven Street, lay the newly buried Otway Burns, privateer, hero of the second war with the British, the War of 1812, a shipbuilder, a North River planter, a Beaufort salt-divvier, brickmaker, tapster. Sailors told tales of him, and Maffitt had heard them: how Burns once reversed course in his longboat when a man on the New Bern waterfront called out that Burns was no better than a licensed robber, how Burns, instead of going on to his ship, went back to the wharf, walked up to the astonished heckler, and threw him straightaway into the Neuse River; how he ended his days as keeper of the Brant Island Shoal lightboat, in the Pamlico Sound well off Portsmouth Island and behind Ocracoke Inlet, wearing an extravagant uniform, drinking the most expensive whiskeys he could get in that way-out-yonder spot, and cursing majestically. Once "the Scourge of the British," now he slept beneath the live oaks with all the rest.

Even at thirty-one the lieutenant knew he held mortality not too far at bay: his own father, who was said to have saved twenty thousand souls, was a few months dead and buried back down south in Mobile. Lieutenant Maffitt felt an urgency within him about the coastal project, as if he could and would sift the sands of all these shores, grain by grain, if time and the gods let him, and know them all just so and make it be that captains and pilots and sailors unknown and never to be known to him could take his

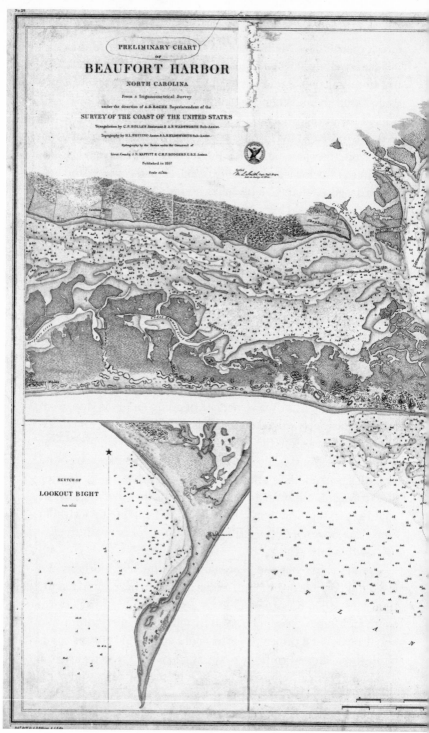

Beaufort Harbor, North Carolina, by a U.S. Coast Survey Party, John N. Maffitt, U.S. Navy, lieutenant commanding

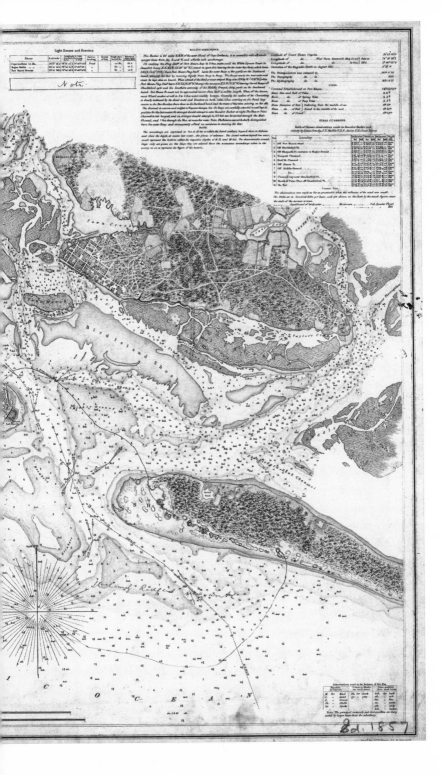

notes, his tables, his charts and make their ways coastwise and into any port whose approach he had plotted and do so with the confidence of Caesar.

Here in Carteret County in North Carolina's central coast, Maffitt sought a system of buoys and beacons and range lights for Beaufort harbor, as he would write Superintendent Bache come February: "With such guides a stranger could enter, day or night, without fear."

Inside Beaufort Inlet

EARLY 1850S

A November storm was building, the breeze freshening steadily. Maffitt had all his canvas furled, and his schooner's lines sang, and she rode the swells hard, pulling at her chains, and he prayed that the *Gallatin* would not drag anchor, even though he knew she would not. He had nearly twenty years of Navy in him now, and he had learned all over the Atlantic and the Mediterranean Sea how much anchor rode one laid out to keep a ship in place. Over the afternoon the wind's speed grew from twenty knots to nearly forty, gusting to fifty. Wild ponies that browsed along the shoal beaches took cover in the short cedars of marshy islands. Planks that might have decked a boat flew by atop rushing waters.

From a schooner riding out the late-fall blow in the channel, he saw little movement along the Beaufort waterfront. Now and again someone would appear to check and tighten dock lines, perhaps to add more. Let a small sailing skiff get loose in such weather and the Lord only knew what damage it might do to other craft, or where it might end up. Skiffs already swamped and sunk in the shallows were the safer craft; for they were all made of juniper and water loved them and would not hurt them, and they could be bailed easily enough in the calm to come.

When the wind-driven rain played through heavily in torrential bands, the lonesome plank houses on Front Street facing south toward the sea—some galleried across their second stories as well as their first—appeared and vanished, vanished and appeared. The gale blew the rain sideways in sheets, wild veils with hanks of smoke behind them, and when the *Gallatin*'s bow fell

Revenue cutter Gallatin *at anchor, Newport, Rhode Island*

(she was pointed into the northeast wind), the sheeting storm ob-
scured not only the houses of the apparitional town but also the
very difference between the craft and the sea herself, so silver-gray
and blinding was it all.

At dawn a brilliant sunrise lit eggshell blue skies, and a rainbow curved across to the west. By noon the waters were flat calm,
and Maffitt could send men ashore for provisions in the ship's
boat, the town having now returned from the spirit world of the
storm, pecan leaves and branches and yaupon sprigs with small,
plump bright-red berries all littering the commons and the sandy
streets. And he could think about getting back to work, sounding
out and charting the undulations of both the shallows and the
deep.

He saw, and knew, the place in all weathers and seasons. Come
June and after a steady, windless rain of half an hour, a south-
westerly storm passed over Beaufort roads at dawn and moved on
off into the sound and marsh country to the east. Maffitt stepped
to the ship's rail and regarded the small port town beyond. Soon

the eastern light would wash over it all, and in small gardens the laden pear trees, rinsed and still dripping wet, would show reds that sailors only see at sunset. Thunder rumbled away to the northeast, and his ship rode and rested easy on her chains.

Pleasures of the harbor, thought Lieutenant Maffitt, and pleasures of the town. Still, the time had come that he must move on down the Carolina coast, reposition his survey party, and tend to the needs of Bald Head Island, the port of Smithville, and the Cape Fear River.

The Wind That Blows, 1850

The country desperately needs another great compromise over slavery, as a dying man needs more than one transfusion. Henry Clay is in the midst of it all again—the new American territories of New Mexico and Utah will be free to determine for themselves how they wish to apply for statehood, whether as free or slave states. California, lately the golden bonanza land, will come in as a free state. A fugitive slave act will require citizen cooperation and federal enforcement in returning fugitive slaves living or abroad in the North to their owners in the South. For this balancing act Clay reels in the support of Daniel Webster, who will be pilloried and vilified by the abolitionists, who have been sold out, they say, like the slaves whose freedom they champion. John C. Calhoun, cadaverous and enshrouded in a hooded cloak, slips into the Senate to hear Webster's speech on the 7th of March, and the Compromise of 1850 soon becomes the law of the land, Clay once again forestalling rift and rent in the national fabric.

Onto the American stage march minstrel shows. Rambling the countryside like the wandering troubadours of old, singing news of intrigue and murder, riddles and mysteries. And yet there is something strange and wondrous about it all: they are telling two stories at the same time, those of the white men performing beneath blackface masks and those of the black men whom the masks portray—the melodies are well-made and catchy, by turns jaunty and poignant, but the lines of the songs make the stage slaves clownish, sentimental, and all in all are a world apart from real black slaves, who never hear, learn, or reflect upon the lyrics of Stephen Foster and the rest who write for the minstrel shows.

It is as if these minstrels sing for a punchdrunk nation, or for a man who no longer knows who he is, like a player onstage who has forgotten his lines or mixed them up, or even forgotten whether he is the actor or the act. If the stage is a mirror, who then does it reflect? The didacts of New England, the fire-breathers of the South? Who has a mirror clear enough to reflect them all and strange enough to do so all at once? Who has the nerve, the hand, the blood strong enough to hold such an instrument?

Senator Calhoun dies on the final day of March 1850—and now he meets the one true Great Nullifier, the one who effaces all. He lies temporarily entombed in a metallic coffin (made by the Yankees of Rhode Island) on the cold, cold Capitol grounds in Washington, till his remains can be shipped south to Charleston. The Calhoun coffin passes through Wilmington, North Carolina, an upriver seaport that is the state's largest city, on Wednesday the 24th of April, at two in the afternoon. The black-bunting-hung steamer *Nina* awaits it and then carries it down the Cape Fear River and out to sea, and yet Calhoun passing in death has touched this place, somehow endowing it with a great role to play—even in death, even on the way back to Charleston, where his good may be interred with his bones. In less than fifteen years, Wilmington will become the last wheel spinning on the wagon of the king, the king whose name is Cotton, whose country is the South.

Maffitt, 1851-1861

Orton Plantation
Brunswick County, North Carolina
AUGUST 21, 1851

At eight o'clock in the evening, Lieutenant Maffitt, commander of the Coast Survey's *Gallatin* now at Fort Johnston in Smithville, arrived on horseback after a ten-mile ride beneath a waning third-quarter moon upriver to Orton, the oldest and largest rice plantation in southeastern North Carolina. Orton was ablaze with lights, the white-columned house and its live-oak grounds brilliant with candles and lanterns everywhere, and the master of the plantation, Doctor Frederick Jones Hill, gave Maffitt—the only attendee new to the place for this evening's soiree—a tour at once.

Clusters of scuppernongs and August floral displays hung all about. The hostess greeted the Navy officer, then rushed to attend to a woman whose apparel was in disarray. Maffitt, who noticed women and they him, certainly noticed that. A cotillion was called and danced at quarter past eight and then, just as the dance ended, fireworks began, four rockets firing off into the night sky, and a gong was sounded, signaling the start of a series of dramatic scenes to be played upon a small stage on the lawn, especially built for this party. Arabic music and its ear-bending quarter-tone scales poured forth wildly from a concealed orchestra, as the guests formed up into an audience, all of them sitting in a Chinese pagoda.

So the evening proceeded. For some hours, habitués of Orton performed scenes from *Pickwick*, *Dombey and Son*, and *The Bride of Lammermoor*, enacted a gypsy encampment and an artist's studio, these short dramas alternating with waltzes, polkas, a curtsy cotillion, a basket cotillion, and a sociable cotillion. Once

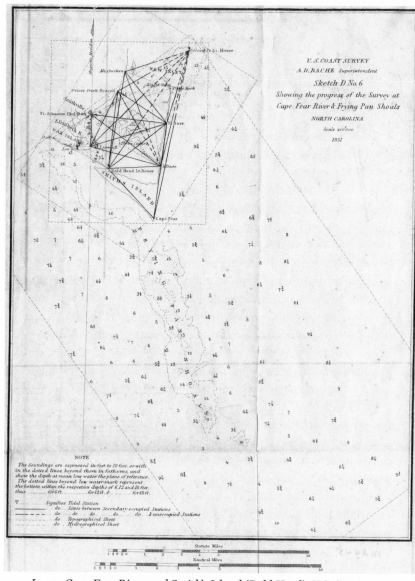

Lower Cape Fear River and Smith's Island (Bald Head), U.S. Coast Survey Chart "Showing the progress of the Survey"

The Gold Diggers played off, the whole company repaired to the house, where fruits and sparkling Epernay awaited them.

At half past midnight, a violin-scored reel featured all the characters from all the skits and sketches dancing together, the evening's final amusement for the guests. At 1:30 A.M., after a farewell from the lord and lady of Orton, back onto his horse climbed the thirty-three-year-old hydrographer for the long trot back down to Smithville. The half-moon hung lazily in the west, and the young lieutenant was far more than pleased; he was a man entranced.

A week passed and John Maffitt took pen in hand, and, as if imbued with the ghost of Sir Walter Scott, described in detail this lavish Orton scene. He mailed his celebratory missive to the *Wilmington Herald*, where it appeared three days later, on Sunday, August 31, 1851, under his nom de plume: Crowquill.

The Theater at Fort Johnston
Smithville, North Carolina
SUMMER 1852

A dress rehearsal played in Fort Johnston's post theater.

Lieutenant Maffitt had started this little theater for the amusement of the men at the fort, his own survey party as well, and for the healthy diversion of the wealthy Wilmingtonians who visited and summered here—if there were no art, no uplift for such a community, he reasoned, its common life would turn to gossip, even scandal. A keen, merry man by nature, Maffitt loved the theater and made a captivating actor—this time out, he was staging the popular farce *Box & Cox*, a drama wherein two men with diametrically opposed work schedules share the same apartment, unbeknownst to them, the plan of an unscrupulous concierge to collect double rent on the same space.

What would that be like? Maffitt had wondered as he first read the script, and, later, as he rehearsed it. *What would that be like at all?*

To have another man, a virtual double—a doppelganger—right in one's own place, one's home, at nearly the same time, but to have circumstances that made the presence of one and the absence of the other synchronous, coterminous, and then, precisely, for the reverse to be true? Why, it makes one doubt, however fancifully, the validity of all that one knows! What happens in familiar places when one is not around and about to bear witness? Or in places that are unfamiliar, exotic, elsewhere, foreign? He began to think about all the things that occurred for good and for ill in the waking world while a man was asleep and in the deep sea of dreams of people both known and unknown to him while he was awake. He mused upon trees falling in the tenantless forest and making sound yet no sound, and even fathomed that mysterious, mystical place all sailors and most landsmen know, the place in the sea where all the lost things wind up, Davy Jones's Locker.

As precise and mathematical as *Box & Cox* was, as funny as it was (and no one liked to laugh any more than John Newland Maffitt did), there was also something about it that made this thoughtful man—so accustomed to taking the measure of the sea in all sorts of places no one had seen, or ever could see—feel by turns quizzical, on the lighter side, and unsettled, on the darker.

"Doesn't it make you wonder?" Lieutenant Maffitt asked one of his fellow thespians.

"Wonder what?" The man was master of the ship's chandlery at Smithville by day, and had supplied properties for the production.

"What occurs behind our backs, as it were," said Maffitt, "when we're off somewhere else."

"No," the chandler said. "Does it you?"

"Why, yes, of course," Maffitt said. "Indeed, it does."

The dress rehearsal now ended, the actors having changed out of their costumes came making their ways toward Maffitt to seek his comment and notes. The chandler left them to him and went back to his props, presetting them for tomorrow's performance, calling back over his shoulder: "A man'd go crazy wondering about such as that all the time, Cap'n. A laugh's a plenty for me."

Ellerslie Plantation
Cumberland County, North Carolina
1852

At St. Paul's Church in Charleston in the heat of Tuesday, August 3, 1852, Lieutenant Maffitt, the sailor and social being already much loved in the city of Charleston for his harbor work, became the beloved of recently widowed Caroline Laurens Read, her late husband also having been a Navy lieutenant, and a friend and associate of Maffitt's. After they were married, during the brief honeymoon the newlyweds took, her three children and his two all stayed with John Maffitt's cousin, Mrs. Eliza Maffitt Hybart, at Ellerslie.

The young newlyweds went to the shore, where Caroline charmed John more than ever: she had brought a bound volume—*Moss Book*, it said on its spine—and she walked on the beach, collecting from tidal pools tiny stems and weblike fronds, little tendrils and filmy panels faint green or maroon in color, seaweed to press and let dry in her book. On its inside front cover, she signed her new married name: "Mrs. Caroline Laurens Maffitt" and the date "Aug 5th/'52," and, just below those words, with pen and ink she wrote down a poem she had memorized:

> Call us not weeds, we are flowers of the sea
> For lovely and bright and gay tinted are we.
>
> . . .
>
> Our exquisite, fragile, and delicate forms
> Are nursed by the ocean, and rocked by storms.

Upon the Maffitts' return, their season turned in a heartbeat from bridal to funereal. Caroline's namesake daughter, youngest of her three, had run too close to a fire in the plantation yard during the children's play and caught her dress afire and died—Ellerslie's people all believed that she breathed in flames and scorched her lungs.

Now the new husband and wife were suddenly bound beyond love, were bonded in grief. They pledged each to each that wherever they should live, Caroline's coffin would come with them, and be buried and reburied, however many times it needed to be in order to stay with them forever.

Was every bond of love and friendship, conceived in even the most devoted of joys, only a bond to sorrow?

Was the sea made salty from the tears of women?

Charleston, South Carolina

Lieutenant Maffitt received a newspaper review of a book, *The Rappers, or, The Mysteries, Fallacies, and Absurdities of Spirit-Rapping, Table-Tipping, and Entrancement,* and, soon enough, a copy of the book itself. One entire chapter was devoted to a series of evenings in which his late father was conjured up by a medium and a circle of devotees: "The Spirit of Rev. John N. Maffitt." His father's spirit, so it was reported, charged one of the communicants at the table with having maligned him, written against him in life, but only to get a good article out of it. Spirit Maffitt then seemed to forgive the man, who had no recollection of the deeds for whose commission he was being blamed: "You newspaper people are the kindest people in the world." Later, the spirit railed: "My friend, I am a preacher. I wish I had ten thousand tongues, and I would undo all the wrongs I did when I lived in your sphere. I could easily identify myself if you remember the scar. I cling to you, as you appear to be a sincere seeker after truth. I am happy to manifest my presence to circles who are unprejudiced and charitable to all. God is merciful to all his children, and before his throne I humbly bow in prayer for all who are willing to be blessed."

From years gone by, Lieutenant Maffitt remembered the histrionic preachings, the swooning crowds, his father being passed hand over hand, all the women throwing jewelry into collection plates, some of them even evidencing the leer of invitation. Then the *National Police Gazette* back in late 1848, accusing him of marrying poor Fannie Pierce in New York, only to take advantage of her for ten days and then throw her over, whereupon she died of a broken heart—"A Reverend Wretch," they called him. And now this. His father in a grave in Mobile, and still this. So many times over, he thought, recalling Doctor Browne's *Urne-Burial* judgment, the good doctor was right: "Oblivion is not to be hired."

On his way down Meeting Street to an evening's fete in his and his shipmates' honor at the Charleston Hotel, he had a hard time getting all this out of his mind—but he did.

The commercial leaders of Charleston were enormously pleased by the years of work Lieutenant Maffitt and his Coast Sur-

Charleston Hotel, Meeting Street, Charleston, South Carolina

vey party had given toward the improvement of both the harbor and the approaches to it—his proposal for "deepening the water over our bar," as they called it, had found many friends. Now the Chamber of Commerce was throwing a big party to honor the survey's people, particularly John Newland Maffitt.

George Alfred Trenholm, president of the chamber, was also the head of John Fraser & Company, shippers of cotton. Trenholm was one of the South's wealthiest men, and his business interests were manifold: he owned plantations, ships, railroads, hotels, wharves, and banks, and he had a grand home in Charleston, Ashley Hall, some miles back from the water, from which he assayed and ran his world. Tonight Trenholm would bestow upon Maffitt one of life's grand honors.

First, at a 4:00 P.M. business meeting, Alexander Bache, the Coast Survey's director, presented a very large chart of this harbor to the Charlestonians. As Maffitt was, and long had been, Bache's star in the field, it was incumbent upon the superintendent to be here tonight, joining in and toasting Maffitt to the heavens. Bache honored the Charlestonians with the chart, saying: "Had it not been for the kind encouragement, liberal indulgence, and warm confidence of Charleston's citizens toward the Coast Surveyors, that map never could have been executed."

Nearly a hundred guests then repaired to the hotel dining room, and the toasts came flowing forth. Henry Gourdin, one of Calhoun's most ardent devotees, saluted the vision and valiancy of the coast surveyors. Old Colonel James Gadsden, who had twice fought the Seminoles, and who only six months ago had negotiated most of fifty thousand square miles away from Mexico in the "Gadsden Purchase," raised his glass to them, and so did Edwin P. Starr, Esquire, subscriber to the great artistry of Audubon. And so, too, did William M. Martin, president of the Farmers & Exchange Bank. A journalist covering the occasion said he wished the entire state of South Carolina might have been there to enjoy the night's "one glowing feeling."

The evening's real surprise, though, was in what Trenholm and the Charlestonians were doing beyond this festive moment: they were renaming the Sullivan's Island Channel, Maffitt's phenomenal discovery, and forever after the city and all the mariners who entered its harbor and touched here would know the road and call it by its new name. A heady night it was indeed: Maffitt was thirty-five years old, two years now married into the heart of Charleston society, or *chivalry* as they deigned to speak of themselves, and as of here and now one of the features of the earth itself carried the good lieutenant's name: Maffitt's Channel.

Furlough

1855–1857

Yet Maffitt's season of gold would not last.

In the spring of 1855, the Trinidadian-born U.S. senator Stephen Russell Mallory of Florida moved in Congress to create a Naval Retirement Board, a bureaucratic implement that would prune the U.S. Navy of dead wood, of officers that the board deemed unfit to command ships of the line, men who should not be at the helm of a man-of-war. Before long, 201 Navy men were publicly announced by the board as being unfit for service, and from a September 1855 newspaper article John Newland Maffitt got the word.

Lieutenant Commanding Maffitt, by now thirteen years assigned to the Coast Survey (at times against his own wishes, as when he had sought to join the squadron for the war with Mexico, only to have Director Bache intervene and keep him from it), was on the Retirement Board's list. At the vigorous age of thirty-six, he was furloughed, detached, and grounded.

Maffitt was astonished, infuriated, and supremely determined to fight this besmirchment—yet it would be nearly two years before he could get a hearing in Washington. Meanwhile, from his home at "Carrieville" on the James River, he campaigned with Bache, and swiftly so. Though placed on the reserve list with furlough pay on September 14, 1855, Maffitt was, on October 13, 1855, by action of the secretary of the Navy, put back in charge of a Coast Survey Party. Hit hard and hurt by the Retiring Board's action, he did what he had always done: Maffitt went to work with vigor and zeal.

He sailed south and checked upon the movements of the North Helena Sound bar, and he sounded all around Fort Sumter in Charleston harbor. He went up the coast and sounded the bars off the Cape Fear River, those migrating at Bald Head Island's point, and the sanding and shoaling at New Inlet just above Bald Head. Far out at sea, he discovered a long chain of undersea hills that ran from Florida to North Carolina down beneath the Gulf Stream. Between June and November 1856, Maffitt studied the James River, recording its shoreline, sounding its depths, from Hog Island to Dancing Point, above the mouth of the Chickahominy River. Aboard the schooner USS *Crawford*, he examined everything from South Carolina's Cape Romain and the entrance to Bull's Bay all the way down to Tybee Light, Georgia.

And he reexamined Maffitt's Channel off Sullivan Island.

Say what they will in Washington, he thought, no one can take that away from me. Or the sea, either.

Washington, D.C.

When Lieutenant Maffitt's day in the monumental city came at last, he chose to be his own counsel. With characteristic vigor he produced and examined in great detail numerous fellow Navy men from his midshipman days, his sailing master and acting-lieutenant days, his surveying days, all of whom vouched for him with profuse praise, and he produced many depositions, attesting the very same, from those who could not attend in person.

Many Navy men—some of whom knew Maffitt quite well, some of whom knew him little or not at all—spoke for him in the hot hearing room, and salt after salt saluted him for, as one said, "possessing energy and ability unusual, and a natural turn, with love for his profession." He drew the highest regard from a civilian, his boss, Alexander Bache, superintendent of the Coast Survey, who was unstinting in defense of John Newland Maffitt in his testimony on the 6th of July 1857:

> As a navigator and pilot on our coast he is not excelled. The amount, accuracy, and economy of his work as a hydrographer have not been exceeded on the Coast Survey. . . . He requested me to let him go with Captain Parker, which I declined. To the gulf also. I considered him so valuable to the Coast Survey that I objected to his leaving it unless he was peremptorily ordered. The secretaries of the Navy, to whom I have stated my positions, acquiesced in them, so that no other order was ever given detaching Lieutenant Maffitt from the Coast Survey. . . .
>
> As my memory runs over Lieutenant Maffitt's career, I see in its general features, and particular details, everything to confirm the judgment of the late secretary of the Navy, who restored him to command, and to stamp him as deserving the highest consideration of the court whom I have the honor to address, in a restoration to the full honors of the naval profession.

Three days later, in a lengthy speech on the 9th of July, Maffitt displayed every ounce of vinegar he was made of. He disputed the few doubts cast against him by commanders who had spent years ashore, when his own naval record showed him never to have lingered ashore for more than a few months at a time. He attacked "the imaginary point of incapability on my part to perform at once, if called on, the executive duties of a ship of war," and he reminded his judges that "the arduous, necessary and all important duties of the Coast Survey are devolved, by a law of Congress, upon officers of the Navy."

Lieutenant Maffitt carried the day and cleared his name. He would have a new naval assignment within a year, though he could not yet know that his time in scientific pursuit of shorelines and harbor approaches, of angles and ranges and ocean bottoms would soon be drawing to a close.

————

Six days before Christmas 1857, aboard the schooner *Crawford* in Charleston harbor, Maffitt wrote Superintendent Bache of changes around Bald Head, arguing for a prolongation of the western Bald Head jetty. He cited James Wimble's chart (he of Wimble Shoals) of 1738. He remarked the sanding up of New Inlet and Zeke's Island, the narrowing of New Inlet between the Atlantic Ocean and the Cape Fear River. He had no wish ever to leave this service, for it came to him that he was just beginning to know, to sense, and almost to *feel* the myriad, confusing, ever-shifting contours of the eastern and southern American deep as well as he knew the design of his own person.

————

Into this moment of John Maffitt's professional melee came another.

A letter from the Reverend James E. Crawford of the Pleasant Street Baptist Church, Nantucket, Massachusetts, advised Maffitt that kinfolks of two of his wife Caroline Maffitt's slaves—Diana and her daughter Cornelia—wanted to buy their freedom. Maffitt wrote him back: "Nothing would give me greater pleasure than to confer upon them the blessings of liberty, provided Reverend Crawford will pay $1,900 at sight." Crawford, who was Diana's brother-in-law, despaired over Maffitt's reply, but soon found funds coming his way from Quakers in England and Scotland and made a deal with Maffitt for Diana's purchase for seven hundred dollars.

By July 1857, Reverend Crawford had quit his ministering at Pleasant Street and was concentrating on raising another one thousand dollars to buy Cornelia from the Maffitts. With help from the well-known New York abolitionist Lewis Tappan, Reverend Crawford got the thousand dollars he needed and soon journeyed to the South to purchase Cornelia and bring her back to the North with him. In February 1858, he did so by train, the black preacher posing and passing as a white master, though his young niece Cornelia, now a free black, was informed by the trainmen that the only way she could go to the North was by riding in the baggage car, as baggage.

Aboard the USS *Dolphin*
Caribbean Sea
1858

John Newland Maffitt was fully restored to grade January 29, 1858.

In the south Atlantic and the Caribbean, as master of the USS *Dolphin* (June 1, 1858), Maffitt would now chase slavers and pirates. Before summer's end, while running along Cuba's northern coast between Sagua la Grande and Cardenas, the *Dolphin* captured the 187-ton brig *Echo*, brought her to by a pair of shots across the *Echo*'s bow and one at her main topsail, and took and boarded her off Cuba on the 21st of August 1858. Her cargo was 318 black African slaves, most of them naked, stowed in a hold the height of which was less than four feet (the ship had left Angola with over 455 captives). Maffitt sent the *Echo* and the surviving Africans into Charleston, South Carolina, under the command of one of his officers, Lieutenant Bradford, and a prize crew, there to await justice.

The *Echo* sat at the customhouse wharves, from which the ship would be sold. Over the Africans (considered by the Federal government free people of color, liberated by Captain Maffitt and the

Dolphin), a legal disputation developed between the sheriff of Charleston District, who believed he could and should seize them for being illegally in the state of South Carolina, and the state's attorney general, who advised him to the contrary that he could not. Dr. D. H. Hamilton, the Federal marshall, ordered the Africans held at Fort Sumter, a U.S. government redoubt, and led a party of observers out to see them: federal officials (a U.S. district judge, the district attorney and Dr. Hamilton himself), lowcountry cotton and rice planters, merchants, and bankers aboard the steamer *General Clinch*, which Marshall Hamilton had engaged to bring the Angolans a bale of blankets, a hogshead of bacon, and four casks of rice (he also promised them pipes and tobacco). In what may be one of the odder theatricals yet in South Carolina history, the Africans, apparently in fine fettle by this time, sang and danced for their white visitors. President Buchanan soon ordered the Angolans returned to Africa, though to Liberia, not Angola, while a jury acquitted the slaver's captain and crew of piracy and set them free.

Even so, Lieutenant John Maffitt's *Dolphin* was the first U.S. ship on this patrol to capture and bring in an active slaver.

Washington, D.C., and Caribbean Sea

1858–1859

Caroline Maffitt fell ill, and she was not faring well at all when Maffitt returned from sea duty and the *Dolphin*. Fearing her malady had to do with miasmas of the lower James River, the Maffitts left their home there, "Carrieville," and bought the house at 1214 K Street in the nation's capital. Visitors at their new home included such distinguished men as Judge Jeremiah Black, Commander Joshua Sands, of course Alexander Bache, and their families. By October 1858, Lieutenant Maffitt was working in the Coast Survey's headquarters office there in Washington, staying ashore and close to home, tending to his ever-weakening wife.

Not long after the turn of the new year, as John Maffitt held her in his arms, Caroline Laurens Read Maffitt breathed her last.

What have I done wrong? Lieutenant Maffitt asked in grief. *Why did such a kind woman deserve to die? Why was I born to lose her?* The children were distraught, both over the loss of her and its effect upon him. Over the months to come, John Maffitt spoke of her constantly, as if he could not let her go.

Maffitt enrolled his daughter and stepdaughter, Florie Maffitt and Mary Read, in Mrs. Kingsford's Seminary, 415 E Street, Washington (where Florie would study piano, vocal, and melodeon music; Milton; and the French Revolution and take a first in the history of literature). He placed his son and stepson, Eugene Maffitt and Laurens Read, under the tutelage of the Reverend Lippitt of Georgetown. The younger children Maffitt sent down to Ellerslie and the care of his cousin, Eliza Hybart.

By the summer of 1859, Maffitt was ordered to serve as commander and purser of a steamer, the USS *Crusader*. At sea that fall, Maffitt learned of the attack by Ossawattomie John Brown and his small band on the Federal arsenal at Harper's Ferry, Virginia. Armed along with Brown fought a free black saddler named Lewis Leary, who had come of age in Fayetteville, North Carolina, and who died in a hail of rifle fire from Federal marines putting down the raid under the command of Robert E. Lee. Maffitt puzzled over the Fayetteville connection when he heard of the raid and of Brown's trial and hanging in December; and he puzzled no less over the plea in favor of John Brown put forth by a Massachusetts man named Henry Thoreau.

Lieutenant Maffitt himself was far away from all this, sailing once more to interdict illegal slavers in the Caribbean Sea.

Aboard the USS *Crusader*

Florida and Caribbean Sea

1859–1860

On May 9, 1860, from Key West, Florida, Lieutenant Maffitt wrote a letter to Florie, sending her his love. Less than two weeks later, on May 22, 1860, he was at sea near the east mouth of the Bahama Channel, off Lotus Island on the Bahama Bank. On May 23, near Nuevitas, he spied a bark showing no name and no colors, and Maffitt overtook her and sent a boat to board her.

As the boat approached, the whole ship before it seemed to

be moaning, like a living thing all in grief. The *Crusader*'s men boarded, and the officer opened a hatch: at once, scores of black men burst out of the hold and flew in tumult about the deck, dancing and singing with wild, exultant joy, climbing on the rails and in the rigging, breaking open bread barrels and water casks, ornamenting themselves with belaying pins tied to their wrists and ladles around their necks. Then came the African women, who gathered and sat off to the side, naked, unabashed, in silence and in tears.

The ship, which would later prove to be the *Bogota*, held 422 Africans and was forty-five days' sail from Whydah in the Bight of Benin, where the king of Dahomey had sold them all into slavery and sent them off to the New World with a French master and his Spanish crew. When the *Bogota*'s captain came aboard the *Crusader*, Captain Maffitt said to him, "You declined to manifest your nationality, sir?" To which the other responded: "I have no flag, no name, no papers—I am a slaver, sir, and now your prisoner."

"Is that all you have to say in reference to this capture?" asked Maffitt.

"That is all, sir."

Lieutenant Maffitt proceeded back to Key West, which, by the end of May 1860, had been deluged by more than fourteen hundred Africans captured by three different Federal ships, including the *Crusader*. Maffitt had freed many of them, pulled them loose from the slavers, yet what they were now free and loose upon was a desert island. Free to play music, to dance and make entertainments for themselves in African tongues none but they understood, and also in this sultry place free to feel its heat, its biting flies, and its malarial airs. Free to die: 294 of them found their last end in unmarked sand graves on a Key West beach, while all three slave captains went free.

Palm fronds clacked together in the gulf breezes. Buzzards sailed and soared above, as their ancestors had been doing, uncomprehending, for ten thousand years. No man's argument or aggression interested these prowlers, only when the dead appeared to them, and then they tilted and canted their broad black wings and circled round and twirled in closer for a look. Then they dropped down and scavenged, while high-piled white clouds in rafts rolled and floated over all, shadowing men, women, children, vultures, and palms from time to time, then rolling on.

By the summer's end, Lieutenant Maffitt had captured not only the *Bogota* but also another slaver, the *Kibly*, on July 23, and a pirate, the *Young Antonio*, on August 14. He cruised the Caribbean and the gulf all fall and was out at sea in November 1860 when Abraham Lincoln was elected President of the United States, and when fear of Northern aims under Lincoln fueled a wild secessionist fervor that spread quickly throughout the South.

As the *Crusader*'s purser as well as her captain, Maffitt had to put in at an American port and procure funds to pay his crew.

He sailed for Mobile, Alabama, to cash his check.

Aboard the *Crusader*, Anchored off Dog River Harbor
Mobile Bay, Alabama
WEEK OF JANUARY 3, 1861

On the quarterdeck Lieutenant Maffitt stood, watching the two visitors he had summoned to his ship come aboard and approach, and then greeting them courteously but coolly. Having learned of crowds in New Orleans recently cheering the departure of one Union ship, he knew that his own vessel was less than welcome here in these waters. Maffitt wore dress blues, and, as commander of a Federal man-of-war, he was at this moment the most powerful representative of the U.S. government in Alabama—he may as well have been the Union itself.

"Good day, gentlemen," Maffitt said.

One of the two, Colonel John Forsyth Jr., was an attorney, was editor of the *Mobile Register*, and had served Mobile as mayor and the United States as minister to Mexico, yet he had already raised a company to fight for the South, should it come to that. The other, Colonel Murrell, was an uncle of Maffitt's first wife, Mary Florence Murrell, the betrayer who bolted from him. Both men were citizens of an Alabama whose militia, under the orders of Governor Andrew Moore, had on the 4th of January just seized the Federal arsenal at Mount Vernon and two other Federal redoubts, Fort Gaines and Fort Morgan in Mobile Bay.

"Good day, Captain Maffitt."

"Good day, sir."

"I have received word," Maffitt said, "that several secessionist boats intend to move upon this vessel, planning to capture her. I want you to carry word back to any and every man who might approach us with hostile intent that should they do so, I will open my broadsides and cut them to ribbons and sink every desperado among them within fifteen minutes. Thank you."

Maffitt did not smile. He shook each man's hand, turned on his heel, and strode back to his cabin. The shipboard interview in Mobile Bay had ended.

Maffitt's message reached its intended ears. Though the U.S. government check he wrote would not be honored by any bank in Alabama, no force came against the Union ship. By the eleventh of January, the day Alabama seceded from the Union, the *Crusader* had already helped resupply several Federal outposts in the Caribbean and was safely anchored back at Key West.

1214 K Street, Northwest

Washington, D.C.

APRIL 29, 1861

Lieutenant Maffitt sat at his upright piano, playing idly upon it, no one else but he in the house. Already he had dispatched his daughter, Florie, and her stepsister, Mary Read, to the South, first to Charleston to meet his brother-in-law, John Laurens, who would see the young women safely on once again to cousin Eliza Hybart at Ellerslie. On the piano he picked out "Yankee Doodle," then, more slowly, "Jeannie with the Light Brown Hair." The sun was setting over Georgetown and the rocks and rapids above it, going down over the Long Bridge and the wooden trestling of the Chain Bridge across the Potomac, and over the Fairfax Rock way to the west, and what sunlight remained was faint in this parlor.

When he left the house for an evening walk, Maffitt was not in uniform but in plain clothes and without his cloak—far too warm for that. He strolled slowly along K Street to the east, then down

Tenth Street toward Pennsylvania Avenue. Maybe he would walk all the way to the Capitol and see how the dome was faring these days.

At the First Baptist Church on Tenth, though, he stopped. He had heard that John Ford of Baltimore might make the big brick building with its arched doorways into a theater. Maffitt would enjoy having a theater here, so close to his home. Less than ten years earlier, Maffitt thought, lingering, he had been an impresario of sorts himself, putting the Smithville players together back down in North Carolina, *Box & Cox* on the boards, and all the other shows that he whipped into shape and that brought some measure of mirth to the little port town.

Washington City was noisy tonight: Union army, horse and foot, flooded the capital, artillery wagons rolling, clattering over the hard dirt streets. Down the hill to Pennsylvania and its young, low oaks Maffitt strode, then the last ten blocks to the Capitol, the second, windowed tier of the dome now finished overtop the first tier's ring of columns. Viewed from a distance, a tall crane stood like a mantis, as if it had risen from within and eaten down the dome that was now not there, devouring it neatly and evenly.

All spring a devouring had been going on. Secessions of the states across the South. Fort Sumter fired upon and taken by the Charlestonians, *Fort Sumter, by God!* Lincoln blockading the entire Southern coast. The open courting of U.S. Navy officers by politicians promoting their new confederacy in the South, and so many friends of Maffitt's resigning and leaving the service. Not Lieutenant David Porter, though, he had not gone over to the rebellion. What had the Navy secretaries promised him? Maffitt wondered. No word of any new assignment for Maffitt, though, nothing since his leaving the *Crusader* in New York, not a word from Secretary of the Navy Isaac Toucey, or, now, from Lincoln's new secretary of the Navy, Gideon Welles.

John Maffitt had gone over everything slowly and slowly made up his mind. In the 1850s, with more than twenty years of service in the Navy, he was wrongly furloughed, called by his inferiors insufficient in knowledge, training, and skills to go on—till he knocked the chocks out from under that argument and brought the best of the Navy and the Coast Survey here to Washington to praise his work and see him reinstated. Now, with twenty-nine years of service, he had defended a ship of the line from being seized by Mobile rebels in the service of Alabama's secession. Now he had sailed the *Crusader*, a serious Federal asset, safely back to the New York Naval Yard (arriving there more than two months earlier, on Saturday morning, February 16), receiving praise from the *New York Times*: "This vessel has been signally successful in capturing slavers, having made three prizes during her cruise." He had invested his own money in the *Crusader*'s necessities and payroll, and remained unrecompensed all this spring by the U.S. government. He had followed his detachment orders. He had returned to his K Street home to await further orders, which never came, and now he felt that hard, unsettling, and disheartening truths about the nation he knew he had served long and well were within his grasp.

What he had heard from several quarters was that the Lincoln government would likely arrest him.

On the 28th of April Lieutenant Maffitt resigned his commission. And now, on the 29th, he had had confirmed from a trusted friend what he already knew, that he was indeed on a secret government list as one to be taken into custody. His offense could only be that he hailed from North Carolina.

So be it.

Lieutenant Maffitt would not be in town this fall to see John Ford's new theater raise its curtain, or to enjoy the run of the Christy Minstrels upon its boards.

Lieutenant Maffitt would slip away from Washington, D.C., inside of three days' time.

Grandy,
August 1842 – January 1844

9 Blandford Place, Regent's Park
London, England
OCTOBER 1842

On the 4th of October 1842, the rap at George Thompson's front door in the Regent's Park, a carriage-set land of villas and terraces, came from Moses Grandy's hand.

Immediately welcomed into the home by Thompson, the black man followed the Englishman into his study, where Thompson sat at a small marbletop table and opened and read the letters of introduction Grandy had carried with him from America. He had sailed from New England the week of August 8, 1842, bound for Liverpool and London by way of New Orleans, his purpose in Louisiana to try to find his children.

And buy them.

Thompson wore a long formal coat with broad lapels, a black cravat around a high collar, dark curly hair and muttonchop whiskers down the sides of his lean face. The letters, written by prominent New England abolitionists — Fessenden, Winslow, and others — could hardly have held higher praise for Captain Grandy.

Wrote one: "I seize my pen in haste to gratify a most worthy coloured friend of mine. . . . His benevolence, affection, kindness of heart, and elasticity of spirit are truly remarkable. . . . Just get him to tell you his narrative, and if you happen to have an Anti-Slavery Meeting, let him tell his tale to a British audience." Another celebrated him as "unsurpassed for faithfulness and perseverance." "A worthy and respectable man," saluted a third. Thompson concurred with his correspondents, and was as immediately impressed with Grandy as the black man had been with Thompson in Boston years earlier. That was when Grandy witnessed a mob storming the hall where Thompson had held forth one night, the latecomers' malice vivid as sin, and then a throng of admirers screening Thompson till he could flee by way of a backstage door. Thompson had come over, about 1834 or '35, to lecture and campaign with Garrison—and though Moses Grandy could not read or write, he could sure enough tell what the signs meant when, outside the house in Boston where both Garrison and Thompson were staying, people during the night had left a diminutive gallows and a pair of full-sized nooses.

For two weeks, over the numerous visits it had taken to get it all down, George Thompson sat at his marbletop table, scratching away with a quill-pen as Captain Grandy spoke out the story of his life. By the 18th of October, Thompson had his manuscript well in hand and had drafted his introduction for Grandy's narrative, and he was moved as he wrote:

> I listened to his artless tale with entire confidence, and with a feeling of interest [in] which all will participate, who peruse the following pages. Considering, his Narrative calculated to promote a more extensive knowledge of the workings of American slavery, and that its sale might contribute to the object which engages so entirely the mind of Moses, namely, the redemption of those who are in bonds, belonging to his family, I resolved to commit it to the press, as nearly as possible in the language of Moses himself. I have carefully abstained from casting in a single reflection or animadversion of my own. I leave the touching story of the self-liberated captive to speak for itself; and the wish of my heart will be gratified, and my humble effort on his behalf be richly rewarded, if this little book be the means of obtaining for my coloured brother the assistance which he seeks, or of increasing the zeal of those who are associated for the purpose of "breaking every yoke, and setting the oppressed free."

Baptist Chapel
Canon Street, Birmingham, England
NOVEMBER 18, 1842

The slender little book—*Narrative of the Life of Moses Grandy; Late a Slave in the United States of America*—appeared in print in

England a month later, and received "Literary Notice" on November 16, 1842, in The *Anti-Slavery Reporter*:

> Anything more touching than this little work could scarcely have issued from the press. . . . He solicits in England further help. The extensive sale of this narrative will aid him most materially, and, in aiding him, will promote the anti-slavery cause. . . . The entire narrative has been thrown into language of beautiful simplicity and purity, so that it can minister no offense to the nicest taste. . . . The book itself is so beautifully got up as to be well entitled to a place in the drawing-room table, among the elegancies of the season.

Two days later, accompanied by Joseph Scoble, secretary of the British and Foreign Anti-Slavery Society, Moses Grandy attended a major gathering of the society's Birmingham chapter. The *London Noncomformist* covered the session and reported that it was a "numerous and respectable meeting of the friends of this society" as well as "other friends of freedom." Joseph Sturge, the Quaker corn factor who founded the society, presided and spoke of a recent journey to the former colonies, during which he said he "experienced no little difficulty in persuading many of our friends in America, that as a class, the coloured race possessed the same intellectual capacities as themselves."

And then Moses Grandy rose and spoke to the assembled. A liberated African, the *Nonconformist* called him, accredited by the antislavery societies in America: he "who had just arrived gives a heart-rending account of the cruelties practised by the planters in the southern states toward their slaves. He himself had been subjected to the greatest oppression and fraud, having purchased his freedom, fixed at 600 dollars, three times in success from his owners before they granted him his liberty. He had arrived in this country for the purpose of raising the means of purchasing the liberty of his child and four grand-children, who had been sold into slavery in the southern states."

So Moses Grandy was now on tour, Birmingham his opening night—and he was well received, his tale seeming to be just the one that these people wanted to hear. They not only made him feel right and justified (he was supremely confident and had always felt so) but also applauded him and what he had to say in a foreign land, and they made him feel important, in a way that was something new.

General Anti-Slavery Convention
Freemasons' Hall
London, England

JUNE 1843

Freemasons' Hall on Great Queen Street had held many a gathering, many a concert and musicale, frequent readings of literature and plays, speeches, lectures, and convocations of the learned societies of the day. Now the abolitionists were to gather here in force. At one end of the enormous hall hung an oil portrait Benjamin Robert Haydon had done of this group's last meeting, titled *The Anti-Slavery Society Convention, 1840*. In the painting, the vast room was thronged with delegates, and Moses Grandy, standing before the gigantic canvas (it was more than nine feet tall and over twelve feet long), noted that the hall was filling again.

Many of these same people must have been here then, he figured. They must have seen the same sight that Haydon's brushstrokes showed: thick-set Thomas Clarkson, the old abolitionist warhorse who had come to his calling as a youth, writing of slavery in Latin for an essay contest he won and thinking himself "almost a Quaker," laying down the Word fiercely (and if he quavered perhaps it was more from the ferocity of the message than from age) as he had for most of his eighty-three years, left hand aloft. And not twenty feet from him sat delegate Henry Beckford, a black man, a freed slave, living, breathing proof and evidence that the world the society envisioned could come to pass, its values prevailing.

Now Moses Grandy would take his own seat amidst the hundreds—from all over England and Scotland and Ireland, and also from France and Haiti and New York, Massachusetts, and Illinois—to watch and listen. Among the American countrymen whose voices he heard were the Reverend J. W. C. Pennington (James Pennington, the slave blacksmith of Maryland, escaped

World's Anti-Slavery Convention, Freemasons' Hall, London, 1840

and become a great preacher of Hartford, Connecticut, the man who joined in marriage Frederick and Anna Douglass) and Lewis Tappan of New York, who with his brother Arthur was among the most reviled men in the American South—it was said that an advertisement in a New Orleans newspaper once offered fifty thousand dollars to any man who would deliver up Arthur Tappan, and that Lewis Tappan had received through the U.S. mail an anonymous threatening letter accompanied by the dry, grisly ear of a Negro.

The convention was to meet for a week, from Tuesday to Tuesday, June 13 through 20.

On Saturday evening the 17th, the society's secretary, John Scoble (the man who had helped Grandy tour about England,

Scotland, and Ireland these many months since they first appeared together in Birmingham), stood and spoke: "I wish to introduce to the Convention Mister Moses Grandy, who had been a slave in North Carolina, and had . . . purchased his freedom three times over at an expense of eighteen hundred dollars."

Moses Grandy rose to the applause of the hundreds of delegates and spectators here in one of the world's largest and most civilized cities, his heart pounding at the joyous recognition this company afforded him, and at the recognition only he could deeply know: *Lord, I am come a very long way from Camden.*

Indeed he had. By the time Moses Grandy was in England, standing before the antislavery convention of the entire *world*, he was faraway and free, he was flying all right, as he had so often dreamed. He was a very long way from canalboats and the Narrows of the Pasquotank River at Elizabeth City and the locks at South Mills and Deep Creek and all those in between. From barrel staves and riving shingles and owls crying and bobcats screaming of a night in the dark juniper depths of the Great Dismal Swamp. A long way from Newbegun and that Christmas morning at Westmoreland plantation twenty years ago. Yet he thought of his old masters: Enoch Sawyer fifteen years dead, William Muse twenty years gone.

Moses Grandy felt more alive than ever, standing here the freest of the free, having outworked, outsmarted, outlasted, and outlived those who had held him in bondage.

Thank you, Mister and Mrs. Grice, thank you, Captain Minner and Mrs. Minner, Mister Garrison, Mister Thompson, even hard old Squire Willie McPherson, dead now, too, I know, yet who, for all he held against our people, made all the difference in my world when he spoke up that one time for me, just that once at Major Farrange's tavern. . . . Thank you, Lord God, for You have let me sail and fly a long, long way from home to be here now. Born hard by the Pasquotank, standing hard by the Thames.

Many rivers to cross, and many an ocean, too.

Praise God amighty, amen.

Liverpool, England

Moses Grandy walked the waterfront from which two steamships would leave with the River Mersey's ebb on August 5: the *Great Western* for New York City and the *Hibernia* for Boston. Grandy had been in the old port of Liverpool for a week at least, awaiting funds from William Lloyd Garrison back in Massachusetts, so that he could sail home aboard the new Glasgow-built sidewheel steamship *Hibernia*. He admired the three-masted, barque-rigged craft, heard talk on the docks that between her engines and the wind she would make nine knots on her way from Liverpool out past the Isle of Man and through the broad straits between Ireland and Scotland, and then off to the north of Ireland, off to Halifax, Nova Scotia, and then on down into Boston.

The ship could accommodate 120 first-class passengers, and these pilgrims would spend their days, when they could, walking the main deck, sometimes in thick mists or rain, sometimes in bright sun. Heavy swells the North Atlantic would provide, and the ship would roll. If the travelers were not sick, they ate well at their dinners: roast beef, goose, breads, cheeses, plum puddings, and currant pies.

In truth, Grandy would be happy to be on either one of the ships, but still he had no funds to cover his passage, and as he waited he could not help but feel an old despair coming on. He sat in a hotel lobby in Liverpool the last week of July and talked out a letter that the hotelier took down for him, a letter to John Scoble back in London: *Where is Garrison's money for me, my steamship ticket money? How else can I make it home?*

Of the Anti-Slavery Convention's other attendees, Joshua Leavitt would be on the *Hibernia*, traveling first-class and arriving in Boston on August 18. The Reverend Pennington would take the *Great Western*, arriving in New York on August 21.

Moses Grandy's name appeared on the passenger list of neither ship.

So how did he make it to New England, to Portland, Maine, or wherever else his family was by now? How, by faith, did he make it home to those he had not seen for a year?

Boston, Massachusetts

JANUARY 19, 1844

In time back in Boston, Moses Grandy visited the abolitionist Oliver Johnson, publisher, friend, confidant, and future biographer of William Lloyd Garrison. There in Johnson's offices at 25 Cornhill Street Grandy gave him, for an endnote in the forthcoming American edition of Grandy's *Narrative*, an accounting of his kin and their costs, his own dealings in the trade in human skin.

The endnote that Johnson recorded as Mose Grandy spoke read simply:

NOTE.

I have paid the following sums to redeem myself and relatives from slavery, viz:

For my own freedom	$1,850
For my wife's	300
For my son's	450
Grandchild's	400
To redeem my kidnapped son	60
Total	$3,060

I now wish to raise $100 to buy the freedom of my sister Mary, who is a slave at Elizabeth City, N.C. Her master says he will take that sum for her. M. G.

New England

1844, IF NOT BEYOND

Once Moses Grandy stepped out of the publisher's office and onto the gray pavers of Cornhill Street, he and his life became a collage of questions.

Where did he go from there?

Back to his family? Had they awaited him in Portland, Maine, all that time he had been gone, from August 1842 till perhaps sometime in August or September 1843, if not later? Or had they returned to their longtime home and awaited him in Boston?

Did he live long enough to see Garrison burn the U.S. Constitution? To see Senator Daniel Webster and learn of his "7th of March" speech in support of the Compromise of 1850 and the further expansion of slavery? To witness the Free Soil and Fremont movement? To learn of John Brown's attack at Harper's Ferry?

Of Abraham Lincoln's election?

Of Civil War?

Of Emancipation?

No one would ever know when Moses Grandy lay down for the last time, or what his last words were before he was laid to rest. Neither the when nor the where of it.

Even when before the law and his fellow man he had been a slave, his was the soul of an emancipated man. He dreamt many times over that he flew, and so, finally, he did. If an honest man is indeed the noblest work of God, as the poet Alexander Pope claimed, then here was one. He kept his end of the bargain, even when bargains failed him twice, and still he kept his end again, till he walked free. Walked, flew, and even more than flew.

In his life's work he was first and foremost a sailor, a supplicant depending upon the motions, and mercies, of wind and water, which still and always abide. From a Pasquotank River ferry-flat and the freightboats on the old Dismal Swamp Canal to the lumber schooners in circuit around the Albemarle Sound to the bluewater ships that took him to the old wine-dark Mediterranean Sea and then around the world to the East Indies, he was a mariner, and he did what mariners do.

Mark it down for all time. Read it as the epitaph for a great man born in Camden County, North Carolina, who lies somewhere in an unmarked grave, its whereabouts known only to the mind of God:

Captain Moses Grandy.
He sailed.

Maffitt,
May 1861 – January 1869

Montgomery, Alabama

MAY 7, 1861

By nightfall on May 2, Maffitt, carrying only a small valise, his compass, and his spyglass, stopped, talked quietly and spoke a few calm words with a fellow officer on the District side of the Potomac River ("Let us hope there'll be no war," he said), then crossed the Long Bridge over to Alexandria, Virginia. For four days he endured thick smoke and cinders playing down onto the train cars, in through their windows and doors, as they went crawling from Alexandria to Richmond, Danville, and Greensboro to Columbia, Augusta, and Atlanta, the cars drawing ever southward to Montgomery, Alabama.

There John Newland Maffitt presented himself to President Jefferson Davis, offering his services to the South's navy. And then, even as it was transpiring, his short visit with the Confederacy's new leader suddenly struck him like something from a dream. "Our friends in the North," said the President, "advise us that there will be no war."

Maffitt was aghast at the ignorance in the room. The men with whom he was meeting, Jefferson Davis and Stephen Mallory— Mallory, of all men he should least like to see, creator of the old Retirement Board that had sought to cashier Maffitt, Mallory now a secessionist and at Davis's elbow, his secretary of the Navy— seemed in no way to grasp just what he was telling them: No war? I have come to you directly from Washington City, where the caissons are rolling, where a great army has been gathering, where Lincoln is planning for war. Whether you are or not. And what do you have for a navy? Two tugboats from South Carolina, frail riverboats in Louisiana that you could knock to pieces with a pis-

The Long Bridge over the Potomac River from Washington City to Virginia

tol shot? A nation with three thousand miles of shoreline cannot do without a real navy. Not in peacetime, let alone in a war.

They appreciated his coming (did they really? Maffitt sorely wondered, noting closely how nervous and suspicious of him Mallory acted). They would find a place for him.

In just a few minutes' time he saw these men as worse than mad, possessed of an invincible ignorance, compounded by vanity and pride. A military man with exquisite training and judgment could not stand to be long in their presence, and so Maffitt, bristling, left quickly.

To his hotel room he strode, walking so briskly, so fueled by pure ire that he was nearly at a run. He packed his trunk, his emotions in riot of anguish, preparing to leave: he would head for Mobile and from there, as best and as soon as he could, sail to England and go to work there and sit out whatever came to pass. He would have no more truck with Davis and Mallory.

Yet there had been friends in the Montgomery room where Maffitt met Davis, men who dared not let him get away—Robert Toombs, Georgia's former U.S. senator, now Davis's Confederate secretary of state, was one of them, Georgian Ben Hill, too, and they had followed close behind Maffitt to the hotel and now stood pounding on his chamber door, till Maffitt admitted them and somberly listened to Toombs's direct, ardent plea.

"You cannot leave the South," Toombs implored him. "Not in her hour of need. You simply cannot."

A man must weigh his life against his losses, John Maffitt thought, the ones already assessed and taken, those not yet incurred but quite imaginable. Maffitt had lost two wives, one to inconstancy and one to death, and in these past two weeks he had left his navy, his life's work, and his Washington home, what property he could lay claim to, all behind him now, probably lost forever. His children awaited him elsewhere in the South. Toombs and Maffitt spoke at length, the traffic of carriages clattering below and the sound of horses' hooves echoing up through the open window. Maffitt again laid out his clear, sensible fear, for he understood entirely the full import of Lincoln's order to blockade the coast: the Union would move sooner than not to close Southern ports and, were there no navy to oppose this, the Union would simply choke the South. Toombs well understood, he said, and warranted the others would, too, in time. As Maffitt listened he heard beyond words the abject earnestness in Toombs's voice, and the timbre of it raised every bit of provincial pride and love in him. Much as he feared the astonishing lack of awareness he had just encountered in Jeff Davis, he feared even more that Toombs was right.

Reared in North Carolina, trained in Pensacola, married in Mobile and then again, and for better, in Charleston, having charted half the Southern coast and sailed it all, Maffitt felt deeply that, the Federal government having failed him, his land was the South and that he might well fail her, as Toombs suggested, should he react in kind to Davis and Mallory and, on the basis of one brief meeting, simply sail away to England.

Toombs had successfully steered the captain from his reason to his heart.

John Maffitt could not, and did not, leave his country.

On the next day, the 8th of May, from Jeff Davis's new nation John Maffitt received a lieutenant's commission, and by the 9th of May, Maffitt was in Savannah, Georgia, assuming command of the *Savannah*, till recently a passenger boat—A more absurd abortion for a man-of-war was rarely witnessed, he thought. By the 6th of June, he was on the way to Norfolk, Virginia, there to collect three dozen thirty-two pounders for Commodore Josiah Tatnall in Savannah, whose command covered the coast from Port Royal to Charleston. Maffitt, thoroughly aware of the full resources and assets of the U.S. Navy, scorned the South's slow movement toward anything resembling a navy of its own. Nothing but passenger craft and old tugs, and cattle boats lightly armed.

Though it was a summer of fevers among the men of Tatnall's squadron, Maffitt wanted to move boldly, and he proposed a host of strategic notions: to destroy the New York Naval Yard; quickly to import huge quantities of guns, clothes, all manner of supplies before a Federal blockading squadron was fully in place; to build a fleet of gunboats; and to convert the twelve-hundred-ton prize ship *Thompson* into a floating battery for Port Royal Sound. All of his proposals were quashed, all but the last, which, he later noted wryly, was "agreed to when too late."

In October, President Davis got word from the North that Union Navy commodore Samuel Dupont was sailing south toward Port Royal with a huge fleet. Earthworks were thrown up hastily, belatedly, on Hilton Head Island, and by the 3rd of November, Maffitt's man in the crow's nest of the *Savannah* shouted down to him: "The ocean is full of ships and steamers!"

Hydrographer Maffitt raised his glass and surveyed his former comrades as, for the next several days, the U.S. Navy sounded and buoyed the approach channel before sailing into the sound in force, which Maffitt knew was inevitable.

Though there was nothing he could do but watch.

On November 7, three Union frigates and fifteen sloops-of-war—Maffitt's old sloop, the *Vandalia*, from the late 1830s among them—moved upon Port Royal Sound and met the resistance of the South's tiny mosquito fleet. Maffitt's *Savannah*, the St. Johns River steamer with a thirty-two-pounder fore and an eighteen-pounder aft, was the best armed of the lot, making it the flagship. When the Union frigate *Wabash* fired what Maffitt could tell was only a *partial* broadside, the mosquito fleet scattered, his own craft taking an eleven-inch shell, which mercifully did not explode, in its mailroom.

The small Confederate craft beat down the coast and ran upriver to Savannah. The whole engagement was over in four hours.

The Federals now owned Port Royal Sound.

NOVEMBER 1861–JANUARY 1862

John Newland Maffitt had shown his mettle, no doubt, yet Commodore Tatnall had not wanted Maffitt to meet the enemy at all, and after a sharp exchange between them, Tatnall relieved Maffitt of his command of the *Savannah* and reassigned him.

Four days later, on November 11, Maffitt appeared at the headquarters of General Robert E. Lee in Coosawhatchie, South Carolina, where he would spend the next two months helping Lee map roads, build forts, and obstruct the upper Coosaw River. There he was stationed and there he stayed—until January 1862, when the *Charleston Mercury* was deeply lamenting the South's "utter want of strength on the water" and declaring "that a navy is absolutely essential," and when his old Charlestonian friend, the merchant, financier, and shipper George Alfred Trenholm came to the aid of the Confederacy by giving the South's fledgling government an unusually swift freighter, a steamboat filled with seven hundred bales of cotton and waiting at the wharf in Wilmington, North Carolina.

Her name was the *Cecile* and the man chosen to captain her

was Maffitt, now a blockade runner, his charge being to take her down to Nassau in the Bahamas and trade that cotton for guns.

Which he did.

Florie Maffitt

LATE SPRING 1862

Four months later, Florie Maffitt, the captain's daughter, sailed with her father out to Nassau upon the blockade-running steamer *Nassau* (late *Gordon*). She was twenty-one now, three years past losing her stepmother, pretty and dark-haired, and very much her own woman. If her father were not afraid, she reasoned, then neither was she—she had been sailing with him since his travels north to Cape Cod in the late 1840s, when she was not yet ten. Disembarking in Nassau on the 4th of May, she took a room at the Royal Victoria Hotel, high on a hill, with all its porches and palms.

And when she sailed from Nassau a few days later (without John Maffitt, who had been ordered to stay and see to his new command, the ship *Oreto*, just come from England), she sat upon the open deck of the *Nassau*, whose hold was now filled with gunpowder. The *Nassau* came under fire from Federal blockaders giving chase, with Florie up on deck vehemently urging the captain not to surrender and insisting that her father would rather her be blown up than see the *Nassau* taken by the U.S. Navy. Florie Maffitt would only be brought belowdecks by orders and coercion, and, watching through her cabin's porthole, she wept profusely when her craft was captured at last.

In New York City, Florie Maffitt, prisoner of war, received every courtesy—for she carried a letter of gentlemanly appeal from John Maffitt to his brother officers in the U.S. Navy, written by her father just in case this eventuality came to pass. After only a matter of days, she was exchanged for some captured Union soldiers and sent back to the South.

Within two years, a new blockade-runner in the service of the Confederate States would, in her honor and for her bravery aboard the *Nassau*, carry the name *Florie*, and it would be her own father who first sailed the ship from England to Bermuda.

Caribbean Sea and Gulf of Mexico

In Nassau John Maffitt took command of the *Oreto*, a sleek two-stacked vessel built in England to be a raider for the Confederacy, after some severe legal jousting. First, a Federal navyman seized her as a prize, but a day later the British admiralty court freed her. She was reseized, then refreed. In early August, Maffitt sailed her out of the harbor, slipping out quietly after midnight, and anchored next afternoon at the remote islet of Green Cay, ninety miles south of Nassau. Another craft, the schooner *Prince Albert*, had surreptitiously slipped in and sailed alongside and brought the necessary martial goods, or so its commander had thought. The heat there was punishing, killing even, and Maffitt's few men (he had 22 when he wanted 130) stripped off all their clothes and loaded the *Oreto* with weapons, with cannon, and transformed her into a warship.

After ten days hard at it, they were done.

Yet, though Maffitt's pivot guns were complete, the *Prince Albert*, loaded hurriedly and secretly back in Nassau, had failed to bring the *Oreto* any rammers, sponges, sights, locks, and the like—her cannon for the time were useless, unable to fire.

Maffitt rechristened the ship the *Florida*, and he very soon realized he had taken on more than a shorthanded crew and cannon that could not fire: yellow fever had also shipped aboard with him.

The *Florida* sailed for Cuba, and the men started falling away. Maffitt was now not only commander of the craft but also her doctor, her nurse. After several days, his stepson, Laurens Read, who had volunteered for this mission, came down with the fever, was wracked by black vomit, and slipped away into the sleep from which he would never awaken. Then the exhausted Maffitt himself collapsed, saying, even as he fell out, "I don't have time to die," and was in the rough grip of yellow fever for a week, while his ship sailed slowly for the Gulf of Mexico.

When Lieutenant Maffitt recovered, he rose weakly to command the *Florida*, many of her guns still either unplaced or unmanned. He resolved nonetheless to break through the Union blockade of Mobile Bay.

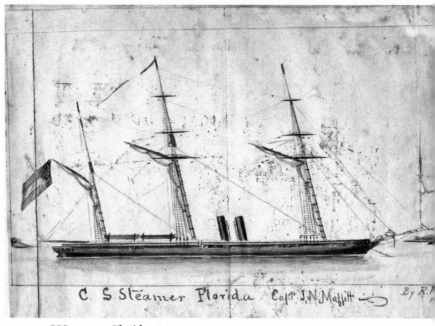

CSS steamer Florida

Maffitt made Mobile Light, and as he approached the bar about 6:00 P.M. on September 4, flying British colors, he was discovered and chased by a pair of swift Union craft, while off to his starboard, U.S. Navy commander George Preble, an old friend of his youth from the *Constitution*, maneuvered his ship the *Oneida* close in. The *Florida* gave no answer to the *Oneida*'s hail, maintained her course after the *Oneida* fired one shot across her bow, still steady on after two shots across her bow.

Maffitt was betwixt and between Union ships at three hundred yards' distance, yet for a moment he had the Federals vexed—vigorous fire from either side, missing the *Florida*, might strike an allied vessel. Still sick with fever and sitting upon his deck because he was too weak to stand (and there on deck alone except for his helmsman), Maffitt ordered the turn of his bow directly at Preble's *Oneida* and steamed at her as if to run her down.

The *Florida* coming hard at him, Preble backed the *Oneida*. Just a bit, yet still just enough.

Maffitt swerved from the *Oneida* at the absolute last moment and was away with the *Florida*, calling his men on deck and aloft to make sail, and now the cannon and grapeshot flew ferociously at him, "a perfect hailstorm of shrapnel," one of the men said, his topmasts and rigging quickly shredded and blasted away. An eleven-inch shell blew a hole in the *Florida*'s side, wounding several men and carrying engineer James Hall's head away. The *Florida* moved forward, northward, Maffitt scarcely giving her a prayer of a chance of getting through. And should she not, well, what else, what more did he have to lose?

Yet get through she did. The Federals—the *Oneida*, the *Winona*, and the *Rachael Seaman*—in their fusillade tore him up badly, though they left his sleek, fast hull intact, if full of shrapnel shot, fourteen hundred balls by Maffitt's later count. The *Florida* was a goer such as they had yet to see. Hard on him as they were, dead-fevered sick as he was, Maffitt still ran quickly out ahead of the Union blockaders and steamed on into Mobile Bay, two hours and eighteen minutes to safety under Fort Morgan, where the men thronged the walls and cheered.

Maffitt had dared the devil, had won the bluff that was no bluff, and had made the most astonishing naval escape yet seen in the Civil War, a feat topping even Matthew Gooding's daring running of the Federal blockade at Beaufort, North Carolina, with

CSS Florida *escaping into Mobile Bay with USS* Oneida *giving chase, September 4, 1862*

John Newland Maffitt, Confederate States Navy, in Bermuda

the steamer *Nashville*. The Confederacy, the country whose president had once declared little interest in any navy, now had her first naval hero, and Lieutenant Maffitt was toasted across the South, from the Chesapeake Bay to Chickasaw Bluffs.

Gulf of Mexico, Caribbean Sea, and Atlantic Ocean
1863

Bristling over the slow, steady pace with which Maffitt repaired and refitted the *Florida* that fall (she had taken "a frightful mauling," Maffitt reported), Confederate secretary of the Navy Mallory summarily removed Maffitt from her command. But President Davis, hearing this, knew he could not afford the demotion of a bona fide Confederate star so soon after his valorous actions, and immediately reinstated Maffitt. On January 16, 1863, Maffitt put fire to his boilers, ran down Mobile Bay and under cover of a gale wind steamed right out past the sleeping sailors of the Union blockader *R. R. Cuyler*.

With the *Florida* finally at full strength, Maffitt now pursued his purpose with a vigor no less than that with which he had once mapped the Union's seas and shores, and that was to raid Union commerce on the high seas. He and Raphael Semmes, commander of the raider *Alabama* (upon which Maffitt's son, Eugene, sailed as midshipman), were to hit the Yankees where it really hurt, out on the shipping lanes. Two craft against fifteen hundred, and they hoped to end the war.

Lieutenant Maffitt captured the *Estelle* as he made for Havana, Cuba, to coal. She was a new brig, valued at $130,000, on her first voyage. Maffitt received Captain John Brown and the crew of the *Estelle* with courtesy, saying to him as the two captains met in Maffitt's cabin: "Sir, I regret that I must burn your ship—the consequences of this unnatural war often fall most heavily upon those who disapprove it."

And then he torched the *Estelle*.

As he left Havana, having taken on Welsh coal, on the 22nd of January 1863 for Nassau, he first captured the sugar-and-molasses-filled brig *Windward* a few miles off Matanzas, set her captain and crew landward on their boats, and then burned her. Before the day was out, he took the brig *Corris Ann*, Cardenas-bound and closing in on her destination, dismissed her captain and crew to their boats, and sent the *Corris Ann* afire and adrift on into port.

But his Cardiff coal was foul. The *Florida* could "make but three knots with it," Maffitt noted. Maffitt jettisoned the coal and now stood for Nassau, which he knew to be "a Confederate strong-hold," and where the hero of Mobile Bay was welcomed warmly at the Royal Victoria Hotel (not a woman there who did not wish to meet him) before he welcomed visitors shipboard. All the while the U.S. consul to the Bahamas fumed over Maffitt's arrival and gracious reception, and the *Florida* took on new coal. Maffitt came out of Nassau standing for New England, chased for a day by the Federal gunship *Sonoma*, which could not keep pace with the *Florida* and fell away from her—he steamed northward, and three days later another Federal craft, an "immense steamer" that Maffitt took for the USS *Vanderbilt*, with fifteen guns, came in close to inspect him in the dark mists of February 5. Down to the deck Maffitt brought his hinged smokestacks, and, with a small light he had hung over his rail, he succeeded in deceiving the *Vanderbilt* into believing the *Florida* to be only "some West India trader." His love of the theater had served him well, and he and his men rejoiced when the big warship sailed south toward St. Thomas.

Maffitt's New England raiding plans were foiled, though, by a hurricane off Cape Hatteras, which sent him well offshore and east of the Gulf Stream with the *Florida*, and he turned south, for he had to coal again soon—the *Florida* could carry only a nine-days' supply of coal.

On the 12th of February 1863, Maffitt moved in upon and captured the Yankee clipper *Jacob Bell*, her cargo sixteen thousand chests of choice tea (as well as spices, silks, chowchow, and camphor) bound from China for England. For the Confederacy, Maffitt took $2.5 million in goods and currency from the *Bell* (said to belong to the abolitionists of A. A. Low & Company of New York), his richest prize to date, and then burned her on the high

CSS Florida *burning clipper ship* Jacob Bell, *February 13, 1863*

seas. Maffitt brought the *Jacob Bell*'s captain, crew, and guests aboard and in one of them, Mary Noyes Williams, a missionary's wife returning from the Far East, he found a sharp adversary: before he put the *Jacob Bell*'s people off aboard the St. Thomas–bound *Morning Star*, Williams had spent five days of desperation and fury aboard the *Florida*, during which she amassed a compelling catalogue of offenses and complaint (plunder of her Chinese goods by the crew, rude gazes from them, condescension disguised as mannerly civility and sociability by Maffitt) that she would publish ere long in her memoir, *A Year in China*. Maffitt, undeterred by her contempt and scorn, considered her a harpie that he was well rid of, and sailed on, prowling.

When Maffitt coaled at Barbados at the end of February, the governor himself invited Maffitt to dinner. "Even the negroes cheered him when he went up the wharf," the *New York Herald* writer wrote bitterly, pegging the Barbadian mood. "Secesh is all the rage. The South is full of glory. The North is bad as bad can be."

Venturing on, Maffitt then captured and burned the *Star of Peace*, bound for Boston from Calcutta, bearing saltpeter for the Union army; captured and burned the *Aldebaran*; captured the bark *Lapwing*, which he kept to use as a tender; captured and burned the ship *M. J. Colcord*, the tobacco-laden clipper *Commonwealth*, the bark *Henrietta* with its barrels of flour and kegs of lard, and the clipper *Oneida*, bound from Shanghai for New York. He captured and burned the brig *Clarence*, and then captured and burned the eleven-thousand-ton, San Francisco–bound ship *Crown Point*. Soon he set the *Crown Point*'s Captain John Giet and his wife and shipmates off on the New York–bound Danish brig *Virginia*, provisioning them with a barrel of bread, a barrel of beef, and sugar and tea. Giet called him "most generous Maffitt."

In May 1863 Maffitt found himself in Brazilian waters, which his fellow raider Semmes and the *Alabama* had also recently haunted. While Maffitt's ship was anchored off Rocas Island, Brazil, for two weeks, the *Florida*'s surgeon, Joseph Dana Grafton, went ashore with several officers. Returning, the ship's boat was upset in the surf. Doctor Grafton grabbed an oar for floating, but, seeing a young sailor who couldn't swim, surrendered the oar to him, saving the sailor's life but losing his own. Captain Maffitt wrote Mrs. Grafton: "It was a self sacrificing heroic act, deeply affecting the hearts of all aboard, who deeply mourned his loss and affectionately honored his memory."

While off Rocas, he also wrote to his children back in Carolina: "I feel happy to tell you that the *Florida* has been doing a fierce business. Up to May 11 she has destroyed $9,500,000 of Yankee commerce, and eluded thirteen Federal men-of-war sent to destroy her and the *Alabama*. . . . I cannot write what my plans are— the duty is very terrible upon one's mental and physical ability; but I am doing all in my power for the benefit of the Confederacy."

Northbound and fiercely so in June, Maffitt captured and burned the ship *Southern Cross*, the clipper *Red Gauntlet*, and the clipper *Benjamin F. Hoxie*. He captured and bonded the whaling schooner *Varnum H. Hill*.

Just off the Hudson River's bar, Maffitt captured the steam packet *Sunrise*, which he bonded, having learned from papers aboard her of the great Southern losses at Vicksburg and Gettysburg just days before. The same afternoon a U.S. Navy sidewheel steamer, the *Ericsson*, sailed down in martial approach toward the *Florida*, yet when the *Ericsson* was within range and Maffitt unleashed a broadside upon her, she immediately turned round and steamed back toward New York without firing a single shot. Maffitt gave chase but lost her in the coming dark and settling fog.

He captured and burned the brig *William B. Nash* and the whaleship *Rienzi*, sloshing with oil and standing for Provincetown. The *Florida* next touched at Bermuda, where she received from the fort at St. George's a twenty-one-gun salute, which she returned. From there, Maffitt sent to Richmond, by way of Captain John Wilkinson and the blockade-runner *Robert E. Lee*, tea and coffee "for the wants of each hospital," as he wrote in a letter, and boots and shoes "for our gallant army." Maffitt then stood to the northeast, capturing and bonding over the packet *Francis B. Cutting* along the way, then capturing and burning the ship *Anglo-Saxon* off Ireland and capturing and bonding another packet, the *Southern Rights*, off England.

In the seven months since he stormed out of Mobile Bay, Maffitt had done in almost two dozen Yankee merchantmen and millions of dollars worth of cargo, a bold, fiery sallying-forth and pressing the cause of disrupting Union commerce so severely that Northern shippers would demand that the Lincoln government sue for peace with the South. Yet now the *Florida*'s engine valves were in bad condition and her driveshaft was out of line. Maffitt's firemen and his engineer warned him repeatedly—he must put in for repairs.

By the time the *Florida* limped into the French harbor at Brest in August 1863, Maffitt and his men were considered by many in the United States and Europe to be the worst scourge of the sea. Some Frenchmen believed anti-Confederate propaganda about

Maffitt's men and their ruthless bloodlust. Coming into port the Southern ship met an anxious, outraged citizenry, a fearful French city where many had heard that the *Florida* sailed with $2 million in gold in her hold, and with the corpses of her victims hanging on her masts, swinging from her yardarms.

None of the gruesome tales were true, and the *Florida*, already a cause célèbre, now became a source of wonder. Her sailors took to the streets, to the taverns and hotels, bought themselves new uniforms, and soon were the talk of the port town. Captain Maffitt and his officers trooped to the theater and were more admired and gazed upon than the show itself—women declared them to be too gallant, too young, too handsome to be guilty of the crimes they were rumored to have committed. The emperor ordered that the *Florida* be repaired and given nonmilitary aid and supplies. Military men from other nations trooped to the waterfront at Brest, wanting to see her, seeking to meet Captain Maffitt, and the English correspondent for the *New York Herald Tribune* gained an amiable audience with him and heard the *Florida*'s tale from its author.

"Won't there be Union cruisers awaiting you when you embark from Brest?" the *Tribune*'s man asked.

"Oh, probably so," Captain Maffitt answered insouciantly. "And it'll be a hard go for a while. But I've run eight blockades already, and, when the time comes, I'll run a ninth!"

So he would, though now was not to be that time for Maffitt: shortly before the *Florida* was to return to sea and resume her career as a raider, Commander Maffitt failed, fell into his bed in his cabin. The mate, alarmed, sent for a French doctor. *M'sieu le docteur* appeared within the hour, boarded the ship, examined Maffitt, and advised him that he had had a heart attack. As the doctor reviewed the captain's history of the past twelve months—the severe yellow fever, the running in and out of Mobile Bay under fire, the tearing about the entire North Atlantic Ocean taking prizes from Cuba to New York to the United Kingdom—he was stunned that his famous patient was still alive.

To stay so, said *le docteur*, he must give up this war.

The fearless Maffitt now stared at this unvarnished truth about himself. He mortally loathed the moment he must stand down from his command, but he did it, writing this news in a letter to Florie, downplaying the problems of his heart as "an annoyance." But he could scarcely play down what he had learned of the war since steaming for Brest, knowing now that Vicksburg and the Mississippi Valley were lost to the South, knowing that Lee had failed on the grandest scale at Gettysburg, knowing now that only the Cape Fear River and the port of Wilmington remained open for Confederate commerce.

Once Maffitt was recovered enough, he accompanied Judge Pecquet du Belley—his newfound friend and French translator, who had smoothed the waters and made all the best arrangements for Maffitt and the *Florida* in Brest—to Paris, planning from there to train northward to Sweden. The tropics had all but killed him, the doctor had counseled—the stringent north-country cold just might help bring him back, trim and trig.

Before he left Paris, though, Maffitt and Judge du Belley dined at the Café de Paris on the Place de la Madeleine, and while in the café Maffitt encountered his own legend face to face. Two Englishmen, strong Confederate sympathizers, sat at a nearby table drinking vigorously and carrying on about the American war, working themselves up, telling each other whom they would like to meet, this general and that cavalryman (they strongly saluted Lee, P. G. T. Beauregard, Stonewall Jackson, James Longstreet), wine fueling their passions, till at last the one to top it all was the man they claimed had just about annihilated the Union's merchant fleet: none, said one of them, could compare with that fellow Maffitt! "I only wish I could see him," he said. "I am told he is in Paris. If I had the good luck to meet him, I'd be damned if I wouldn't call for the very best bottle of Veuve Clicquot!"

And then they were standing, raising glasses, clanking them together, toasting, almost roaring as they cheered, "To Maffitt, to Maffitt, Commander John Newland Maffitt, Prince of Privateers!"

Judge du Belley was looking forward to the champagne, but Captain Maffitt, calling for his bill, could scarcely get out of the café swiftly enough. He was still weak from his heart attack, and he did not want that or any other weakness perceived, seen, known, or exploited. He had also just drunk a glass of wine, and he would not have any word of drinking to go forth about him. If Maffitt were to be unbothered, undiscussed, unmolested, and unknown, he would have to get a good deal farther away from the war than this.

To Scandinavia

LATE 1863

For the first time in his life, John Maffitt had next to nothing to do, no responsibility other than to travel and come to a certain place and then travel on to the next. He longed for the ports of northern Europe, of Copenhagen and Stockholm, and he found them and yet was unsatisfied, for arising out of the business of their wharves and quays and forests of masts a dismay came toward him, as if a reproach over his relative inactivity. Maffitt wanted a helm, and he ached to hear the voice of command well up from within him. Some days, not knowing what was truly happening along the Southern coast back home nearly drove him to distraction, and he knew there was nothing healthy about a man roaming foreign lands feeling disconsolate and of no use, and, even worse, like a man without a country. Only for so long could he stand this—he must go to England, find the Confederate agents there, and arrange to go back into service and back to what he knew, and to what he knew he must do.

The *Florie*, a blockade runner built in Clyde River, Scotland, awaited him, and by January 1864 she would put him back into the martial maritimes.

Aboard the *Lilian*

Bermuda to Wilmington, North Carolina

EARLY JUNE 1864

Six hundred and seventy-four miles lay between Hamilton, Bermuda, and Wilmington, North Carolina, and Captain Maffitt now took command of the blockade runner *Lilian*, a five-hundred-ton paddlewheel steamer, intending to thread the needle once again, his ninth attempt at running a Federal blockade. Among his shipboard guests he counted the Englishman Francis P. Lawley, a former member of Parliament (and horse-racing and gambling aficionado, which was what had made him "former"), who was covering the American Civil War for the *London Times*.

Maffitt departed on the high tide of a moonless night and was assaulted early the next morning, but only by flocks of flying fish. Ere long he spied the masts of a distant ship, smoke swirling around them—he feared a Federal trap, yet he knew he might be wrong and that this could be an innocent vessel afire. Declaring, "No luck can betide a vessel which leaves a comrade in distress at sea," he headed the *Lilian* for her. When it turned out to be a Federal cruiser, billowing white smoke from Cumberland coal, Maffitt quickly turned away and proceeded toward Wilmington.

He was a portrait of calm, and caution. His steam he blew off underwater. At night, no cigar or pipe was allowed on deck—no light must show from the *Lilian* whatsoever.

Next day a tall-masted Federal steamer with huge paddlewheels, coming seaward from the direction of Wilmington, bore down upon the *Lilian* and fired shot after shot at her. All fell wide of their mark. Maffitt built his pressure, soon had his paddlewheel turning at thirty-three revolutions a minute, and steamed away from his pursuer, now toward the inner ring of thickly packed black Federal blockaders.

Night fell. The *Lilian* passed close in, moving almost noiselessly through the blockaders within pistol range of cruiser after cruiser, though all hands were expecting any moment the Drummond lights, the fierce calcium-white limelights high atop their masts, to flash on and allow point-blank fusillades to tear her up.

Yet she came through safely. Soon, though, she closed in upon a Federal launch on the bar near Fort Fisher, a craft that quickly fled rather than pursue the *Lilian*. From the ocean Maffitt spoke up to comrades in the fort on its mound, then slid in through New Inlet and onto the Cape Fear River.

"It is at such moments that you realize how paramount is the influence of a dauntless chief upon all around him; and it is felt more in so confined a space as the deck of a ship than in a great battle on land," Lawley would later write of this passage for the *Daily Telegraph*.

Lilian running the blockade into Wilmington, North Carolina, with Captain John N. Maffitt looking through binoculars at left on sidewheel box, early June 1864

Upon the *Lilian*'s safe arrival in Wilmington, blue-water seaman Maffitt unexpectedly found brown-river orders awaiting him.

Plymouth, North Carolina

SUMMER 1864

No sooner had the *Lilian* reached Wilmington in early June than Secretary Mallory ordered Captain Maffitt up the coast to Plymouth, North Carolina, on the Roanoke River near the head of the Albemarle Sound, where he was to take command of the ironclad steamer *Albemarle*—the key now to the defense of Plymouth, as it had been key to that riverport's recapture from the Federals two months earlier, in the spring. The Confederate ram *Albemarle*, afloat in the Roanoke River, was guarding and holding this all-important choke point and protecting the Wilmington & Weldon Railroad bridge—an essential link in the supply line from Wilmington's wharves to Lee's army in Virginia—sixty miles upstream from Plymouth.

Maffitt was coming to a dark, difficult corner of Carolina, more than he knew and perhaps more than anyone would allow, for a bloodletting in the springtime had left a curse on this place even deeper than the curse of war. When the Confederates retook Plymouth (the Union having held all eastern Carolina's sound and riverports since 1862), the black troops who had fought and lost on the Union side of the battle ran off, routed and retreating into the swamps over the river from town and below it (Peacock Swamp, someone said). Soldiers in gray—three companies horse, one foot—chased them and hunted them down and shot them wherever they found them. None of the victors treated the black troops as enemy soldiers to be captured and made prisoners of war—they were unlucky men out of munitions and on the low end of the wrong side, and Confederate rifles cracked away in those swamps all the day of the Union surrender—April 21. As many as six hundred men may have fallen before them.

To this Southern spot came Maffitt, the ocean sailor, the blockade-runner and raider, a man of constant motion and action. From the time he reported on the 25th of June, the question that raged around him and up the chain of command above him was whether or not to turn him loose on Federal gunboats out in the Albemarle Sound. Mallory wanted to send him out, but all others—in Plymouth, Petersburg, and beyond—were afraid any attack Maffitt mounted would be doomed and would lose the *Albemarle*—both ship and sound—to the Union.

So for nearly three months Maffitt sat in Plymouth, while the political wrangling went on above. And he chafed. As daring as he had been all through the war, he was now nothing more than a river guard, and his craft—a warship at anchor resting on her chains behind a log boom—was merely a floating battery, which meant she was also a classic target. Once, at least, he got some of his men out into the open waters of the sound—he had his pilot J. B. Hopkins (who knew these waters as a packet master from

COAST CHART No. 40

ALBEMARLE SOUND

N. CAROLINA

WESTERN PART

FROM THE PASQUOTANK RIVER TO THE ROANOKE AND CHOWAN RIVERS

From a Trigonometrical Survey

under the direction of A.D.BACHE Superintendent of the

SURVEY OF THE COAST OF THE UNITED STATES

Triangulation by W.M.BOYCE and J.C.NEILSON Assistants

Topography by J.C.NEILSON & J.J.S.HASSLER Assts.

Hydrography by the parties under the command of

Lieuts. Comdg W.P.McARTHUR. JAMES ALDEN & T.J.JENKINS U.S.N. Assts.

Published in 1860

Scale 30000

141   25
7   1860

Western
Albemarle
Sound

before the war) take twenty sailors east and hunt down a Union mailboat, the *Fawn*, capture her (and a Federal congressman in the bargain) at Coinjock on the Albemarle and Chesapeake Canal, and then burn her to the waterline.

And that was it. There he sat, in charge of an impressive, motionless beast, and there in the still August heat, as fishhawks swooped down and worked the lower river, he received word that Admiral David Farragut had damned the torpedoes and, charging through a minefield set out to destroy him, taken Mobile Bay for the North. Maffitt stood upon the *Albemarle*'s deck staring downriver and at the island's forest wall across the way, thinking of all the hot action with the *Florida*, breaking the Union blockade both going into Mobile Bay and coming out, and felt a keen lamentation over where he was just now and over all that he was unable to do with what he had. Farragut is fighting a war, he thought, while I am not.

On September 9, to his very great relief, Commander Maffitt was detached from the *Albemarle*, ordered back to Wilmington,

CSS ram Albemarle

Destruction of CSS ram Albemarle, *Roanoke River at Plymouth, October 27, 1864*

and given command of the blockade-runner *Owl*. Seven weeks later, on the night of October 27, Union lieutenant William Cushing (daring, or reckless, depending upon who was speaking of him) boated up the Roanoke River and found the *Albemarle* tied off hard to the Plymouth wharf with a log pen thirty feet out from her. Cushing laid a torpedo up under her decking's metal plates, set it off, and sent her to the riverbottom. Maffitt was down on the Cape Fear River, his fears realized and very many a nautical mile away.

Wilmington, North Carolina

OCTOBER 1–2, 1864

Captain Maffitt had been in Wilmington only a couple of weeks.

On Saturday, October 1, he learned early of the dispatch just come upriver to the city that morning to Mrs. Armand John De-Rosset (Eliza Jane Lord DeRosset), president of the Soldiers' Aid Society, advising her that the sidewheeler *Condor*, though having successfully run the blockade and being bound in for New Inlet, had then wrecked just before dawn a half mile off Fort Fisher. A lifeboat bearing two passengers and two crewmen headed in toward the breakers and the beach at first light, a strong nor'east wind driving them, and it swamped in rough seas and sank.

Only three of the four survived.

The woman who drowned in the heavy surf—dragged under by the weight of eight hundred gold sovereigns she had sewn into her petticoat, and then washed up on this Southern seabeach—was the voluptuous Rose O'Neal Greenhow, the famous Confederate spy, who had been imprisoned by the Union and, released on an exchange of prisoners, had then gone abroad to raise funds for her country. The gold she carried upon her body for the Confederacy from England to Halifax and then on to North Carolina had carried her instead to her death.

Wilmington received this news like a shot to the heart.

To have lost another blockade runner, and above that to have lost this heroine of the cause—the nor'east wind behind the *Condor* and Mrs. Greenhow was an ill one indeed, and the omens these losses portended were the worst they could possibly be.

On Saturday afternoon the steamer *Cape Fear* drew nigh at the Water Street wharf in Wilmington, and, once docked, yielded the body of Rose Greenhow into the arms of the Soldiers' Aid women, who bore her to the chapel at Hospital Number 4. There, with an honor guard attending the chapel door, she would lie in state. The ladies stopped at nothing: the dead woman was laid out upon a Confederate flag-draped bier and covered in flowers, many of them fashioned into crosses, her head at rest upon a small white pillow with a tatted pillowcase. A crowd formed outside the chapel, and, once the Soldiers' Aid ladies had placed and lit two hundred candles all about the corpse and given the word to the guards, more women flooded into the room, weeping as if the deceased were a member of their families. A sister, an aunt, and children filed in with many of the women to see Mrs. Greenhow, who appeared to the youngest of them to be only asleep, yet the older children knew that was not sleeping. Because everyone about them was crying with abandon, the children cried, too, and a tall ebony cross towered over them all. The mourning proceeded apace until 2:00 P.M. on Sunday the 2nd, when the encoffined Rose Greenhow, the Confederate flag still with and about her, was borne from the chapel to the Catholic Church of Saint Thomas.

In this Gothic hall down on Dock Street, Captain Maffitt joined the throng of mourners and payers of respect. Wearing his gray uniform, his sabre and sash, he stood alongside many another man who had made way for a woman to sit. "Mrs. Greenhow was a hero," said the Reverend James Andrew Corcoran; "she was a patriot; she was devoted to the end." The day's torrents drove down upon the roof and its steep gables and blew hard and noisily against the tall lancet arches of the windows, and the reverend had to speak as forcefully as he was able in order to be heard over the constant crying and the storm. "Let all be warned, though, of the frailty and mutability of all that humankind wills and desires. Nothing is certain. Nothing is certain except the grave. We must have faith in Our Lord and in the better days of redemption and resurrection He hath planned for us and that await us beyond all this that we now see and know. Amen."

Afterward, hundreds of Wilmingtonians followed the carriage with her coffin and her flag a mile up Market Street away from the river, turning north and on out into Oakdale Cemetery, where upon a slope beneath overarching live oaks her coffin was lowered into her grave. As it disappeared into the earth, sun rays suddenly broke through the storm clouds, and the mourners gasped at their brilliance and at a distant rainbow that now graced the sky. As they departed the graveyard, many were tempted to find and read something good in these new lights that appeared late upon what had been such a dark day.

Captain Maffitt knew otherwise.

A change in the weather was just that and that only—there was no good meaning in a drowned woman and a sunken ship in wartime. Yet he could not speak what was in his heart at this moment, for the premonitions were too dark. (In less than a week, Maffitt would receive word that his former command, the *Florida*, was rammed and captured by the USS *Wachusett* during the darkness of early morning in the neutral waters of Bahia, Brazil. In little over a month, he would learn of General William T. Sherman's leaving Union-occupied Atlanta and burning his way across eastern Georgia.) Now, he left Rose Greenhow's grave in Oakdale and walked the mile back down Market Street to stand on the wharf, and for some hours alone just watched the Cape Fear River and its never ending flow down to the sea.

Flight of the *Owl*

At last, on the 21st of December, Captain Maffitt in Wilmington received onboard the sleek speedy steamer *Owl* (she was 230 feet long and could make sixteen knots) a cargo of 780 bales of cotton. He then ran down the Cape Fear, the river now long familiar to him, past Dram Tree Point and Campbell and Keg and Battery islands, the faint lights of Smithville and Fort Caswell falling away behind him as he rode the river flow and met the sea again and once again threaded the blockade, outbound for St. George's, Bermuda. Arriving there on the 27th, he found the port clogged with blockade-runners, all laden and ready to head into Wilmington, all waiting to find out about the fate of Fort Fisher and the recent Union assault.

In the second week of January 1865, a steamer from Halifax brought in this news: between December 24 and 27, the Federals under Major General Benjamin Butler, a sly politician but no fighter he, had sought but failed to subdue Fort Fisher. Butler floated in and blew up a munitions-filled craft on the beach below Fisher, thinking this would collapse the fort, though the explosion had so little effect the Confederates scarcely noticed. The great redoubt was still in Confederate hands, Wilmington was still open, the South still a nation though with only this one outlet to the sea and the world.

Six blockade-runners, the *Owl* under Maffitt among them, along with her sister ship the *Stag*, now set to sea at once. Unbeknownst to them, though, during their two-days' sail a Federal armada under Admiral David Porter and General Alfred Terry began pounding Fort Fisher with a supernova bombardment, attacking and overpowering it in bloody hand-to-hand combat, then captured it at last.

Whoever thought the Federals would return in only three weeks, and with such unmitigated might?

When Maffitt steamed the *Owl* in close to the North Carolina coast at Lockwood's Folly on January 16, the word he heard from land was that Fort Fisher was intact. He quickly moved up the shoreline and steamed past one blockader, past the line of breakers on the channelside bar, and into the mouth of the Cape Fear River. Why were fires burning on Bald Head Island? Why was he getting nothing back from Bald Head for his signals, as he normally did?

Maffitt made for Fort Caswell, tucked up and off to the west side of the river's mouth.

Captain E. S. Martin, chief of ordnance at the fort, ran down to the wharf, startling the night herons from their piling tops. He rowed hurriedly out to the *Owl* and called to Maffitt: "Fort Fisher is in the hands of the enemy." As was Fort Caswell, very nearly. Spying Union gunboats approaching in the distance and knowing Caswell, too, would soon be lost, Maffitt fled the trap and turned the *Owl* out to sea. Even as he did, the Confederate general Braxton Bragg was already laying plans to torch all the cotton bales then sitting on Wilmington's wharves, and the very wharves themselves, to keep any of them from being of use to the Union forces already bound upriver.

Maffitt sailed down the coast into South Carolina waters, past Pawleys Island, past the mouth of Winyah Bay and Cape Romain, standing for Charleston, even though he knew the old port was more heavily blockaded now than at any time during the war. Later that night he neared Maffitt's Channel, still bristling over the *New York Tribune*'s having called it "one of the rat holes to Charleston" back in '62. In the night's haze he nearly rammed a Union blockader, the haze lifting just in time for Captain Maffitt to see the other vessel, order hard aport, and miss the enemy craft by a scant twenty feet.

"Heave to or I'll sink you," the blockader ordered Maffitt, who kept right on, taking a punishing broadside for his disregard. Maffitt's quartermaster, fearing imminent capture, acted on the captain's earlier orders and chopped with his hatchet the rope that held two bags of Confederate government mail out over the water—in one of them Captain Maffitt's journal of his command

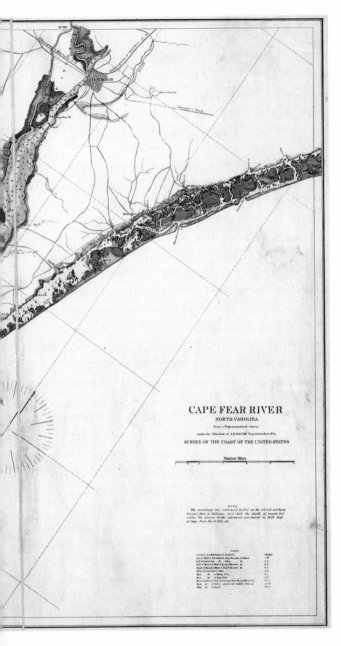

Cape Fear River, from Wilmington to the Atlantic Ocean

of the *Florida*. Other blockaders set to firing and lighting up the night sky, as Maffitt, his forecastle shot through and bulwarks forward of his engine room torn up, got away in the night, once more to sea.

So it went all down Georgia, down Florida, and on around the Gulf Coast, Maffitt prodding, testing, prying, but finding Federal craft everywhere, and nothing Southern remaining open to him and the *Owl*.

Nothing till Galveston in mid-April.

There, a week after Lee's surrender at Appomattox, Maffitt ran in and beat a sixteen-vessel blockade, though the *Owl* then grounded on Bird Island's shoals, well within range of Federal fire. And there she sat, taking shot and shell till Captain James McGarvey, commander of what little was left of the Confederate fleet, now hiding out in Galveston harbor, brought the gunboat *Diana* and her crew out to try and refloat the steamer. One of those accompanying the rescue party would later write of his first encounter with the now legendary Maffitt: "We expected to find him fixed up with gold lace &c., but it was not so. He looked more like a cool, unconcerned passenger than a Captain in the C.S. Navy, with a Scotch cap, a torn coat, and a pair of rubber shoes, without socks."

The people of Galveston clambered to their rooftops to watch. One of Maffitt's sisters was among them, as Captain Maffitt himself gave orders to his own men and to McGarvey's, too, from the *Owl*'s bridge, till at last they succeeded in pulling her off the sand shoal and she floated free again. The *Owl* then made the last delivery of outside goods to the Confederacy.

After Galveston, the *Owl* touched at Havana, Cuba, on May 9, where Maffitt to his surprise found his lifelong friend, former shipmate, and now fellow captain Pembroke Jones. They sailed together on to Halifax, Nova Scotia, where Jones disembarked and they parted. By July 14, Captain Maffitt reached Liverpool, England, anchored in the River Mersey, and, obeying the last order he would receive from the Confederacy, turned the *Owl* over to the Liverpool-and-Charleston-based shipping firm of Fraser, Trenholm and Company.

Sitting in Liverpool, Captain Maffitt then learned in full how the Southern dreams of liberal terms in defeat had been dashed: the full tale of Lincoln's assassination at Ford's Theatre at the hand of John Wilkes Booth, whose bootheel spur raked across the portrait of Washington as Booth leapt off balance from the Presidential box; of the Confederate cabinet's flight by train from Richmond south to oblivion, Jeff Davis in rueful disbelief and George Alfred Trenholm sitting nearby with his feet upon the last gold ingots of the Confederate treasury; of Lee's surrender to Grant, Johnston's to Sherman—Maffitt heard it all. The South was occupied and subjugated, and Maffitt knew he could not go home again, not yet or anytime soon, and he swore he could never swallow a bitter, pardon-taking pill. For a spell he would have to stay on in England, the land where he had come so very close to sitting out the Civil War, but for how long? Now he surely was a man without a country, and certainly a man without funds. If he were going to stay at work as a seaman and again command a vessel of his own, he would now have to gain a new license in this new land, and do so as a British captain.

And so he did—for two years thereafter, Maffitt sailed between Liverpool and Latin America as captain of the British merchant steamer *Widgeon*.

New York Harbor

MAY 23, 1867

On the steamship *Merrimack*, departing from Rio de Janeiro in winter and arriving in New York City in springtime, John Newland Maffitt returned to the United States.

Six long years since he was last upon the waters of the great harbor, he remembered, when he had brought the *Crusader* in during early 1861. The longest years of his life. Adventure aplenty, and no less ruin—he had had two years to reflect on all that, as he sailed and saved, counting his coin by the shilling and the pound, and knowing the thrill of a pence, more or less. Now, he wondered briefly what sort of reception he might get from his old comrades, his antebellum friends, more recently his sworn wartime foes, out at the New York Navy Yard in Brooklyn if he should pay a call, yet he took a bold chance and strode in among them, and he was surprised, stunned even, at the warmth with which they greeted him. John Maffitt could not have known till that very moment the regard in which he was held, a widely held admiration to which even Admiral Porter would later give voice, calling him "a thorough master of his profession," a man who "made no enemies among those officers who had once known him and who now missed his genial humor in their messes"—"he was capable of the greatest heroism, and though he was on the side of the enemy, his courage and skill were worthy of praise."

On this May day, Navy officers seeing Maffitt for the first time in years were all wanting to hear, from his side, of the *Florida* and her exploits, her famous escape into Mobile Bay, the works, and some (those who recalled his daughter's capture and his letter and her release from New York in 1862) even wanted to be remembered to Florie. When he left Brooklyn at last, he was still marveling over the graciousness with which they sent him on his way to his family, bidding him safe travels back to the South:

> The War is over, old friend.
> Welcome home, old friend.
> Welcome home.

On the Wrightsville Road

Wilmington, North Carolina

JANUARY 26, 1869

Down the long gray lane through tunnels of overarching live oaks, Captain Maffitt drove the buggy, the horse's hooves in a muted rhythm trotting over the sand. He was bringing his young companion, Miss Emma Martin (sister of his son Eugene's wife, Kate), out for a few days to visit the rest of the Maffitt family at the captain's farm, The Moorings out on Wrightsville Sound—the ground that Florie, now married to Joshua Wright of Wilmington and this place, had helped her father find upon his return.

His return, indeed: Maffitt had come back to more changes than he ever may have dreamed, and some he may never have imagined even in dreams. Why, the black Union spy Galloway—

who knew this coast so well he had told the Yankees where to land—now served in the North Carolina Senate, a runaway slave now running the state! And here was Maffitt himself, changed or trying to change from sailor to farmer, when he knew full well that a man brought up to the sea was good for little else. Well. The War was over, so they said.

The weather breezed up and the sky darkened quickly, but, before the gathering storm opened up on them, Captain Maffitt slowed and reined in the horse and drew his old dark blue leather cape around Emma and she smiled at him.

"If only this cape could tell its tales," she said.

"There'd be no shortage," said Captain Maffitt, "for I've had it since I was a boy."

The first few heavy drops fell, and, in the premature gloaming the thunderstorm cast over the way to Wrightsville, this middle-aged man and this young woman were about to find a moment of the heart all to themselves. Perhaps they knew the moment was upon them even then, perhaps not—but they would know it in a trice. Who could ever say what kind word or motion in the sensual life of talk and gestures suddenly separated a pair of people from the horde and turned them loose as lovers, each to each only? This one instant, Captain Maffitt's placing the cape around Emma's shoulders, was, finally, for them all that it would take.

Over the objections of her family (her father would write to Maffitt of older men and younger women in matrimonial alliances being "a standing curse in the family for over one hundred years" and that he could not bear Emma's becoming her own sister's mother-in-law), Emma Martin would soon marry the great mariner (on November 23, 1870, at her family's home, 412 Market Street), and together they would have three children. She would help him set down and publish his stories of the late war and of his many years before that with the U.S. Navy (in a novel, *Nautilus, or Cruising under Canvas*). She would support him in creating the Carolina Yacht Club, which would put on sailing races in the sound, and she would work the soundside farm with him and make of it a market garden whose produce and fruits and flowers (potatoes, turnips, apples, peaches, figs, pears, strawberries, blackberries, and raspberries, grapes of all varieties, scuppernongs, arbors of climbing roses, even flax) were renowned in the long, broad Wilmington peninsula between river and sea. And years later she would nurse him—after the early deaths of his grown children, Florie and Eugene, after a President would not clear him to run the Federal customhouse on the Cape Fear River—through his own demise, of Bright's disease, which would break him and send him to the insane asylum in Raleigh, and to his own last end, then, in old Oakdale Cemetery in Wilmington beneath more live oaks, close by many other fallen champions of the old, passed-away South, Emma would bury him.

Surely all this would come to pass.

Yet now they were just a man and a woman alone on a lonesome road in the Carolina lowlands in the rain, as it fell and broke through the live-oak canopy and poured down on the horse and the carriage and the couple.

"You might not guess," said the captain, "that the cape that just now shelters you once kept sea spray off the queen of Greece." Then as the horse pulled them forward through the storm, carriage wheels shushing through wet sand, Emma Martin led John Maffitt, son of Neptune, on deeper into his story with her unending smile and her shining eyes and a single word: "Oh?"

And for a few simple seconds they were apart from all the world, as the storm pelted down in sheets and waves, covering the countryside, the river and its old port town well behind them now and the vast marshes and the sound just ahead, and cloaking it all, as if horse and wheels and man and woman and moment were lingering and could not and would not stop doing so, but remained there hidden forever even after the worst of the storm had passed, beneath the vaulted live oaks and behind a deep and unparting curtain of mist.

Epilogue

Two captains from Carolina ply the great, legendary waters of the world, the North Atlantic, the Mediterranean, the Caribbean, and many others less known, perhaps, but no less important: the Albemarle Sound, the Pasquotank River, the Cape Fear. For the most important water, the most valued craft, to the mariner must be the one he is on at the moment. Moses Grandy's lumber schooner is as dear to him in his transit of the Albemarle, or the *James Maury* on his round-the-world sail, as John Maffitt's surveyor schooner *Gallatin*, or his raider *Florida*, are to him, many years later.

These men might well have served on ships passing each other some night or nights on the Mediterranean Sea. They might have grazed each other's shoulders as they crossed the same streets in Boston in the 1830s. How they do circle each other for years afloat and afield, crossing each other's tracks in ports both great and small in the American East, even in England.

And in the South.

One must purchase his way out of this land and bondage, which is all it offers him, time and time and time again. The other, shirked and suspected by the national regime, is drawn and, he must also feel, virtually forced back into the South as his familial land becomes a new, doomed nation. The South has let one go and she has taken one back: the two captains have changed places.

Their names abide. In time, in the late 1890s, a cousin descended from those who once owned Moses Grandy leaves the family name that served both white and black on a post office and crossroads in Currituck County, North Carolina. In time a craft called a liberty ship is christened the *John Newland Maffitt* and launched (on August 4, 1943) by North Carolina Shipbuilding in

Wilmington for the U.S. Navy, a mile from where the man himself lies buried.

Grandy and Maffitt are known to us as men of great skill on many waters, and those who wander down to the edge of the land and there regard the inscrutable pacings of the rivers and the sounds and the sea will remember these extraordinary men for that, and will marvel no less at what the Fates made of their lives, till at last letting their cables slip, their ships drift before the wind that blows, each of them outward bound, each crossing the bar that one final time.

Two Captains from Carolina A Chronology

YEAR	GRANDY	MAFFITT
1789	November–December: In Fayetteville, North Carolina ratifies the U.S. Constitution, joins the union, and charters the University of North Carolina.	
Ca. 1791	Moses Grandy is born in Camden County, N.C., a slave of William Grandy, then of William's son James Grandy, who inherits him.	
1790s	Grandy's brother runs off and dies in the woods.	
1793	The digging of the Dismal Swamp Canal begins.	
1800	The Pasquotank County Court liberates 36 slaves.	
1801	The Pasquotank County Court liberates 19 slaves.	
1802	At 10 or 11 years old, Moses Grandy is hired out to a succession of men.	
	Supposed Tom Copper Slave Insurrection is being planned in northeastern North Carolina swamps. Slave Mingo gives a deposition against the planners. Six black men are tried in court and found not guilty. Mingo has his ears cut off for perjury.	
	The rate of slaves being emancipated in Pasquotank County falls in years to come.	
	Mid-May: Insurrection fears rise in Camden, then in Currituck, Hertford, Halifax, and Pasquotank Counties.	

YEAR	GRANDY	MAFFITT
1805	Shingle flats begin using the Dismal Swamp Canal.	
1810	September: Yellow fever strikes Elizabeth City.	
1812	Charles Grice, merchant and shipper, erects two batteries at Cobb Point on the Pasquotank River; he is in charge of defending Elizabeth City from the British.	
	December 26, 1812: The Chesapeake Bay is declared to be in a state of blockade by the British.	
	During the War of 1812, Grandy becomes a successful freightboat captain, moving boats on shares via the Dismal Swamp Canal between the North Carolina port of Elizabeth City and Virginia's Hampton Roads, earning and saving money of his own.	
1814	The first ship makes passage on the Dismal Swamp Canal.	
1810s	The merchant Charles Grice, with whom Grandy is working, suggests to Grandy that he use his earnings to buy his freedom, beginning a process that ultimately will take three attempts to succeed. James Grandy, Moses's first owner, lets Moses buy his freedom, then cheats him, disregarding the $600 payment that Moses has made, and then sells him for $600 to a man named Trewitt.	

YEAR	GRANDY	MAFFITT

1818   President James Monroe tours the Dismal Swamp Canal and dines with Enoch Sawyer, customs commissioner at Camden and owner of Grandy's wife.

1819   John Newland Maffitt is born aboard ship from Ireland to New England.

Ca. 1820–22   Grandy's owner Trewitt fails, having mortgaged Grandy to William Templeman Muse, clerk of court of Pasquotank County, who owns Grandy only briefly, selling him to Enoch Sawyer of Camden.

1823   July 19: William Templeman Muse dies at his plantation Westmoreland near Newbegun Creek, southern Pasquotank County.

1820s   Grandy moves between boat work and field work; in being flogged, he receives a serious wound to his side that heals badly and troubles him for years. At one point, Grandy moves into a lean-to shanty on the shores of Lake Drummond in the Great Dismal Swamp to recuperate. Captain Edward Minner of Deep Creek buys Grandy from Enoch Sawyer and, once Grandy repays him, sets Grandy free, after which he spends time in Providence, R.I., and, ultimately, moves to Boston.

1824   Maffitt is taken in and adopted by his uncle, Dr. William Maffitt, to be raised at Ellerslie, a farm near Fayetteville, N.C.

YEAR	GRANDY	MAFFITT
1825	The supposed Edgecombe County, N.C., Christmas Insurrection plot takes place.	The marquis de Lafayette arrives in Fayetteville by horse-drawn carriage.
1827	Enoch Sawyer dies; Edward Minner dies.	Maffitt is sent to boarding school in the North, Professor Swinburn's White Plains (N.Y.) Academy.
1830	David Walker's *Appeal* arrives in North Carolina. Governor Owen sends a copy to the legislature. Panic ensues, the patrol system is strengthened, and more discretion in actions is given to patrolmen.	
1831	August: The Nat Turner slave uprising occurs in Southampton County, Va. Panic ensues in eastern North Carolina that fall.	
1832	Grandy sails aboard the *James Maury* from Boston to Batavia.	Maffitt, 13, becomes acting midshipman in the U.S. Navy on the *St. Louis* (West Indies).
1835–38		Maffitt sails to the Mediterranean on the *Constitution*.
1836	Grandy speaks before a New England Anti-Slavery Society meeting in Boston.	
1838		June 28: Maffitt passes midshipman examination; October 16: assigned to the packet *Woodbury*; November 20: assigned to the sloop of war *Vandalia* (stationed in Pensacola, Fla.).
1839		March 11: On the *Vandalia*, when an officer is cast from the ship by a gale, Maffitt becomes acting lieutenant. October: Maffitt is attached to the *Macedonian*.

YEAR	GRANDY	MAFFITT
1840	Grandy and his household appear on U.S. Census rolls living as free blacks in Boston's Second Ward.	November 17: Maffitt marries Mary Florence Murrell of Mobile, Ala., in her hometown.
1841	Grandy reports living in Portland, Maine.	Maffitt's father, Reverend J. N. Maffitt, becomes U.S. House chaplain. February 6: Maffitt is ordered to Pensacola Navy Yard. October 26: Maffitt becomes acting master of the frigate *Macedonian*.
1842	Late summer, early fall: Grandy goes to England, carrying letters vouching for him from prominent New England abolitionists. There he records his narrative.	February: Florie Maffitt is born; she is baptized aboard the *Macedonian* by the ship's chaplain. April 20: Maffitt is assigned to the U.S. Coast Survey, where he will serve for more than fourteen years, commanding one of the survey's USN ships and doing hydrography of the U.S. coast, rivers, and sounds.
1843	After the publication in November 1842 of the *Narrative of the Life of Moses Grandy; Late a Slave in the United States of America*, Grandy tours England successfully. June 13–20: Grandy attends the General Anti-Slavery Convention in London. June 17: He is introduced by British and Foreign Anti-Slavery Society secretary John Scoble to the convention (also present are Reverend J. W. C. Pennington and Lewis Tappan). Late July: Grandy is in Liverpool at a hotel awaiting an early August ship to return to United States.	

YEAR	GRANDY	MAFFITT
1844	January 19: Grandy is in Boston, seeing to the American edition of his *Narrative*, whose publisher is Oliver Johnson, a friend and ally of Garrison's. No further trace of Moses Grandy exists, no date of death.	
1850		May 28: Reverend Maffitt dies in Mobile, Ala. Maffitt's charting includes work in the areas of Cape Fear, Cape Lookout, and Beaufort Inlet, N.C. He lives in Smithville (now Southport) in the early 1850s.
1851		June: As commander of the schooner *Gallatin*, Maffitt arrives in Smithville, N.C.
1852		August: Maffitt marries his second wife, Caroline Laurens Read, in Charleston, S.C., at St. Paul's. They live in Smithville in a house at Fort Johnston.
1853		Maffitt moves to James River.
1854		June: The Charleston Chamber of Commerce gives an appreciation dinner for Maffitt et al., hosted by George Alfred Trenholm, planter, shipper, and banker.
1855		Maffitt and others are furloughed by a congressionally created Retirement Board.
1857		July: In Washington hearings, Maffitt defends and clears himself.

YEAR	GRANDY	MAFFITT

MAFFITT

1858 — Maffitt is restored to grade and given command of the USN ship *Dolphin*, charged with chasing pirates and slavers in the Caribbean. The *Dolphin* is the first ship to capture a slave ship, the *Echo*, which Maffitt sends to Charleston, S.C.

1859 — Maffitt is given command of the screw steamer *Crusader*, Cuba station, and captures the slaver bark *Bogota* the next spring.

1861 — Early January: In Mobile with the USN man-of-war *Crusader*, Maffitt vigorously stands down secessionists who want to capture it. Later in the spring, in Washington he sees Federal preparations for war and hears of secret arrests of Southerners and of a list of officers from the South who may soon be arrested. Maffitt sends his family to the South, resigns his 29-year naval commission, and follows in early May, making a clandestine passage across the closed "Long Bridge" over the Potomac. Maffitt goes to Alabama, where he offers his services to the Confederacy. After the Battle of Port Royal Sound, he joins Robert E. Lee as naval attaché at Coosawhatchie, S.C., to help with the defense of Savannah. June–August: The slave ship *Echo*, rechristened as the Confederate privateer *Jeff Davis*, sails from Charleston and captures 9 Union prizes in 7 weeks.

YEAR	GRANDY	MAFFITT
1862		Maffitt is assigned to George Alfred Trenholm's *Cecile* to run the Federal blockade from Wilmington to Nassau. He assumes command of the English-built raider *Oreto*, renames her the *Florida*, and, although he and his crew are wracked by yellow fever, breaks through the Federal blockade and enters Mobile Bay, a naval incident of enormous consequence on both sides of the conflict.
1863		Maffitt's *Florida* escapes capture; Maffitt burns and/or bonds nearly two dozen Northern merchant vessels before heart trouble forces him to relinquish command at Brest, France.
1864		Back in action, Maffitt captains the blockade runner *Lilian*, the ram *Albemarle* in the area of Plymouth, N.C., and the blockade runner *Owl*.
1865		After the fall of Fort Fisher in January, Maffitt turns away from what had been the last open Southern port, Wilmington, N.C., and finally gets the *Owl* in at Galveston, then heads to Cuba, Nova Scotia, and finally England.
1865–67		A mariner in England, Maffitt captains the *Widgeon* between Liverpool and Latin America.
1867		Maffitt returns to New York City, is welcomed at New York Naval Yard, then travels to Wilmington, N.C., where he settles at The Moorings, a 212-acre farm on Wrightsville Sound, just east of Wilmington.

YEAR	GRANDY	MAFFITT
1870		June: Maffitt sails the steamer *Hornet* from Wilmington to New York City for the Junta Central Republicana de Cuba (with headquarters at 71 Broadway). November 23: Marries Emma Martin, his third wife, in Wilmington.
1871		Maffitt publishes his autobiographical novel, *Nautilus, or Cruising under Canvas*; during the 1870s, he writes, farms, and sails the sound.
1883		September 28: Maffitt's daughter, Florie Maffitt Wright, dies.
1885		Maffitt is refused a Wilmington customs post by President Grover Cleveland. In economic straits and suffering from Bright's disease, he breaks down and is hospitalized at the N.C. Insane Asylum in Raleigh.
1886		January 12: Maffitt's son, Eugene Maffitt, dies. May 16: Maffitt dies and is buried at Oakdale Cemetery, Wilmington.

Selected Sources

These basic works and resources on Moses Grandy and John Newland Maffitt were constant companions as I wrote this story: Grandy's *Narrative*, spoken to and recorded by George Thompson in October 1842 in London, where it was published shortly thereafter (with the American edition appearing in January 1844 in Boston), available at http://docsouth .unc.edu/fpn/grandy/menu.html and in *North Carolina Slave Narratives* (2005), edited by William L. Andrews; John Newland Maffitt's autobiographical 1871 novel, *Nautilus, or Cruising under Canvas*; his widow Emma Martin Maffitt's 1906 biography of him, *The Life and Services of John Newland Maffitt*; and the Maffitt Papers, Collection 01761, Southern Historical Collection, Wilson Library, University of North Carolina at Chapel Hill (Tim West, curator).

Concerning the 1790s–1820s period, comprising Moses Grandy's early years in northeastern North Carolina, William A. Griffin's *Antebellum Elizabeth City* (1970) has been an essential text on the town, Pasquotank County, and the area at that time, as has Lemuel Sawyer's *Autobiography* (1844). More information on Charles Grice, William T. Muse, Enoch Sawyer (Lemuel's brother), and other figures of that day mentioned by Grandy comes from Griffin's work and from the North Carolina State Archives. Information on Moses Myers comes from the Chrysler Museum of Art, Norfolk, Virginia. The Kinnakeeters incident is based on an anecdote in Ben Dixon MacNeill's coastal classic, *The Hatterasman* (1958). David S. Cecelski's authoritative work, *The Waterman's Song* (2001), explores Grandy's story and is a godsend to all students of coastal Carolina. The location of Westmoreland, Muse's plantation, is described by Mary Weeks Lambeth, who lived there in her youth, in her *Memories and Records of Eastern North Carolina* (1957), a work to which an October 2005 *Metro Magazine* piece by Carroll Leggett led me; Westmoreland plantation lay just below Newbegun Creek in an area of Weeksville now bounded by N.C. 34, Esclip Road, Ramsey Road, and Griffin Swamp Road; a lane (now called Lions Club Road) has long run north-south through this land, and where it jogs slightly at its midpoint, there once sat the big house.

Researcher James E. Ward Sr. searched for Moses Grandy and Edward Minner in early nineteenth-century Norfolk County, Virginia, records at the Library of Virginia in Richmond; microfilm there (of College of William and Mary originals) of the *American Beacon & Norfolk & Portsmouth Daily Advertiser* contains Minner's obituary (issue of September 3, 1827). Shipping news in the *Salem (Mass.) Gazette* reports on the *James Maury*, Captain Woodbury (or Woodberry), the ship upon which Grandy sailed to the East Indies; she sailed from Boston to Batavia (present-day Jakarta) in both 1831 and 1832 (issues of September 23 and October 11, 1831, and September 18, 1832). The lay of the Boston that Grandy and Maffitt knew comes, in the main, from *Mapping Boston* (2001), edited by Alex Krieger and David Cobb with Amy Turner; particularly useful regarding the wards is Plate 35 in George G. Smith's *Plan of Boston Comprising a Part of Charleston and Cambridge* (1835). Grandy's appearance at the third convention of the New England Anti-Slavery Society is noted in its *Proceedings* for 1836, published by Isaac Knapp (Boston), available at the Samuel J. May Anti-Slavery Collection, Cornell University, Ithaca, New York, http://ebooks.library.cornell.edu/cgi/t/text/pagevieweridxc=mayantislavery;idno=02817311;view=image;seq=1.

The New Orleans scene Grandy encountered on his way to London in 1842 is based on reports from Ned Sublette's *The World That Made New Orleans* (2009). The *London Noncomformist* reviewed Grandy's *Narrative* on November 16, 1842, and covered his Birmingham, England, appearance on November 30, 1842. Letters to John Scoble concerning Grandy's travels in England in 1843 (MSS. Brit. Emp. s. 18 C20/106-109 and s. 18 C17/86) were transcribed and sent to me by Lucy McCann, archivist, Bodleian Library of Commonwealth and African Studies at Rhodes House, Oxford, England. The *Proceedings of the General Anti-Slavery Convention, called by the committee of the British and Foreign Anti-Slavery Society, and held in London from Tuesday June 13th to Tuesday June 20th, 1843* were published by John Snow (1843) and may be found at http://www.archive.org/details/proceedingsofgenoobritrich.

Additional information about the 1843 convention's venue came from Susan A. Snell, archivist and records manager, Library and Museum of Freemasonry, Freemasons' Hall, London. Concerning Moses Grandy's descendants, Eric A. Sheppard's *Ancestor's Call* (2003) is of interest.

Rob Hoch of the White Plains (New York) Historical Society provided me with a report on the academy there that young John Newland Maffitt attended prior to his appointment to the U.S. Navy. His many assignments and movements—to Pensacola, the Caribbean, Boston, and the Mediterranean and for the Coast Survey—during the 1830s, 1840s, and 1850s are charted in Emma Maffitt's *Life and Services*; both Caroline Laurens Maffitt's honeymoon *Moss Book* (1852) and a newspaper clipping about the June 1854 Charleston Hotel party for Maffitt, attended by Alexander Bache and other notables, are in the Maffitt Papers at UNC. The story of Maffitt and the abolitionist purchase of one of his wife's slaves comes from William B. Gould IV's *Diary of a Contraband: The Civil War Passage of a Black Sailor* (2002). A useful document concerning Key West and the pre–Civil War interdictions of the slave trade that Maffitt participated in is *History of the African Cemetery on Higgs Beach, Key West, Florida,* by historian Gail Swanson: http://www.afrigeneas .com/webbbs/attach/d/23/23111_1.pdf.

Maffitt's U.S. Navy work against the slave trade (1858–61) was well noted in contemporary newspapers of record, as were his Civil War Confederate States Navy exploits (1861–65), in papers both North and South. The 1864 voyage of the blockade-runner *Lilian* under Maffitt is based on Francis Lawley's report, included in Emma Martin's *Life and Services,* and Rose O'Neal Greenhow's October 1864 funeral in Wilmington is drawn from her papers at Duke University, Durham, North Carolina. Maffitt has been a popular subject for twentieth-century authors, chief among them Edward Boykin (*Sea Devil of the Confederacy,* 1959), Royce Shingleton (*High Seas Confederate,* 1994), and Lindley S. Butler (*Pirates, Privateers, and Rebel Raiders of the Carolina Coast,* 2000).

Other significant, helpful works and resources include *The Graveyard of the Atlantic* (1952) by David Stick; *The Civil War in North Carolina* (1963) by John G. Barrett; *The Civil War in Coastal North Carolina* (2001) by John S. Carbone; *Elizabeth City, North Carolina, and the Civil War* (2007) by Alex Christopher Meekins; and the *North Carolina Maps* online collection, http://www.lib.unc.edu/dc/ncmaps/, a joint project of the North Carolina State Archives (Dr. Jeffrey J. Crow, deputy secretary, North Carolina Office of Archives and History); the North Carolina Collection, Wilson Library, UNC Chapel Hill (Robert G. Anthony, curator); and the Outer Banks History Center, Ice Plant Island, Manteo (KaeLi Schurr, curator).

Acknowledgments

Out of a summertime conversation with Sonny Williamson and Captain Dennis Chadwick this work grew. We were sitting on Lida Piggott's porch, looking across the Straits between the Down East mainland and Browns and Harkers Islands in Carteret County, North Carolina, back in 2005, and we were speaking of the N.C. mariner who was raised on Browns Island and whose life and career Sonny chronicled in his *Captain Matthew Gooding, Blockade Runner* (2001). Further encouragement of this project has come from many up and down the Southern coast: Alton Ballance of Crew's Inn and the N.C. Center for the Advancement of Teaching, Scott Bradley, and James Barrie Gaskill, all of Ocracoke; Captain Ernie and Lynne Foster of the Albatross Fleet, and Joseph Schwarzer of the N.C. Maritime Museum, all of Hatteras; Jimmy and Karen Amspacher of Marshallberg; Barbara Garrity-Blake and Bryan Blake of Gloucester; Scott Taylor and Lenore Meadows, Jeff Adams and Trish Holland, and Carl Spangler, all of Beaufort; *N.C. Literary Review* editor Margaret Bauer of Greenville; Alex and Elizabeth Albright of Fountain; Feather and Willy Phillips of Fort Landing; Jan DeBlieu and Jeff Smith Deblieu, and Tom White, all of Manteo, also Robert Perry and Lindsay Dubbs of the University of North Carolina at Chapel Hill's Albemarle Ecological Field Site there; George and Blair Jackson, Don and LuAnne Pendergraft, Peter and Sue Thomson, Frances Bounous and Rob Powell, and Susan Hinkle, all of Elizabeth City; former longtime Dismal Swamp Canal Welcome Center director Penny Leary-Smith of South Mills; George Ramsey Sr. of the Virginia Canals & Navigation Society; Barbara and Wilson Snowden of Currituck; Lucinda and John MacKethan of Raleigh; Jack and Martha Betts, formerly of Raleigh, frequently of Oriental, now of Meadows of Dan, Virginia; my fellow Coastal Cohorts Jim and Patricia Wann of Tybee Island, Georgia, and Don Dixon and Marti Jones of Canton, Ohio; the late Linwood Taylor of Hampstead and Wilmington; my cousin Nancy Meekins Ferebee of Camden; my aunt Jean Simpson Sharp of Nags Head; my beloved mother-in-law, the late Patricia Cary Kindell of Beaufort; and my beloved mother, the late Dorothy Page Simpson of Chapel Hill, born in Wilmington.

A Chapman Family Fellowship at UNC Chapel Hill's Institute for the Arts and Humanities helped me to start on this book, and the Bowman & Gordon Gray Professorship Program at UNC Chapel Hill supported my work on it as well, including research travel to Boston, where Moses Grandy lived and worked and shipped out on the *James Maury*, and where John Newland Maffitt studied as an acting midshipman before shipping out aboard the USS *Constitution*.

At the University of North Carolina Press, project editor Paula Wald and design and production manager Heidi Perov have again devotedly brought my work to fruition. My editor and publisher David Perry, who has floated the Scuppernong River, Bull's Bay, the Albemarle Sound, and the Northwest Prong of the Alligator River with me, has seen me off on many waters well beyond those, upon some of which David Cecelski has paddled stoutly while slowly sifting with me through all of this story.

Captain Jim Rumfelt took us on a grand sail out of St. Thomas on his craft *Salty Shores*, around St. John's and through the Sir Francis Drake Channel, familiar cruising grounds to Maffitt and many another nineteenth-century mariner.

Jim Byrum and Jane Oliver gave me world enough and time to study the lower Cape Fear River, where it flows into the Atlantic Ocean, from high up on their Old Baldy Lane rooftop overlooking the channel beside Bald Head Island.

Jerry Leath Mills, outdoorsman extraordinaire and by now longtime denizen of the Pamlico River at Washington, North Carolina, yet again brought his most thoughtful literary and editorial acumen to bear on the final manuscript. Jake and his wife, Rachel, an accomplished painter and poet, have kindly hosted me in their home numerous times when I was abroad in eastern Carolina.

And as with all the other voyages, my wonderful, ever-inspiring wife, Ann Cary Simpson, master mariner of my life, has been on this one the whole way.

My deepest gratitude to one and all. Steady as she goes.

MBS III

Illustration Credits

96   U.S. Coast Survey Chart of Beaufort Harbor (1857). Courtesy
       of North Carolina Maps, North Carolina Collection, Wilson
       Library, University of North Carolina at Chapel Hill (Jason
       Tomberlin, public services librarian).

99   Photograph (1855). Courtesy of U.S. Coast Guard (Scott
       Price, deputy historian); Newport (R.I.) Historical Society
       (Jennifer Robinson, collections assistant); and Naval Historical
       Foundation (Frank A. Arre, photo lab manager; Caitlin
       Schettino, historical services assistant).

104   U.S. Coast Survey, "Sketch D No. 6, Showing the progress of the
       Survey at Cape Fear River & Frying Pan Shoals" (1851). Courtesy
       of North Carolina Maps, North Carolina Collection, Wilson
       Library, University of North Carolina at Chapel Hill (Jason
       Tomberlin, public services librarian).

109   Photograph by George N. Barnard (1865). Courtesy of U.S.
       Library of Congress, Washington, D.C.

126   Painting by Benjamin Robert Haydon, *The Anti-Slavery
       Convention* (1841), oil on canvas. © National Portrait Gallery,
       London (Elizabeth L. Taylor, picture librarian).

132   Courtesy of U.S. Library of Congress, Washington, D.C.

138   Painting (1862). Courtesy of Maffitt Papers, Southern Historical
       Collection, Wilson Library, University of North Carolina at
       Chapel Hill (Matthew Turi, manuscripts research librarian;
       Tim West, curator).

139   From *Harper's Weekly* (November 15, 1862). Courtesy of School
       of Journalism and Mass Communications, University of North
       Carolina at Chapel Hill (Stephanie Willen Brown, director, Park
       Library; M. Megan Garrett, assistant, Park Library; Morgan
       Ellis, special projects editor; Speed Hallman, associate dean for
       development and alumni relations).

140   Photograph by S. W. Gault. Courtesy of Lower Cape Fear
       Historical Society, Latimer House, Wilmington, North Carolina
       (Candace McGreevy, executive director; Colleen Griffiths,
       archivist).

143   From *Harper's Weekly* (March 21, 1863). Courtesy of School of
       Journalism and Mass Communications, University of North
       Carolina at Chapel Hill (Stephanie Willen Brown, director, Park
       Library; M. Megan Garrett, assistant, Park Library; Morgan
       Ellis, special projects editor; Speed Hallman, associate dean for
       development and alumni relations); and Wilson Library (Keith

Longiotti, university library technician; Fred Stipe, head, Digital Production Center).

150 From *Illustrated London News* 45, no. 1268 (July 16, 1864). Courtesy of Mary Evans Picture Library, London (Mark Vivian, picture research manager).

152 U.S. Coast Survey, "Coast Chart No. 40, Albemarle Sound, N. Carolina, Western Part" (1860). Courtesy of North Carolina Maps, North Carolina Collection, Wilson Library, University of North Carolina at Chapel Hill (Jason Tomberlin, public services librarian).

154 Sepia wash drawing by R. G. Skerrett (1899). Courtesy of the Navy Art Collection, Washington, D.C.; U.S. Coast Guard (Scott Price, deputy historian); and Naval Historical Foundation (Frank A. Arre, photo lab manager; Caitlin Schettino, historical services assistant).

155 From *Harper's Weekly* (November 19, 1864). Courtesy of School of Journalism and Mass Communications, University of North Carolina at Chapel Hill (Stephanie Willen Brown, director, Park Library; M. Megan Garrett, assistant, Park Library; Morgan Ellis, special projects editor; Speed Hallman, associate dean for development and alumni relations).

160 U.S. Coast Survey Chart of the Cape Fear River ("The survey of the entrances was made in 1858, that of Cape Fear River 1851–1853"). Courtesy of North Carolina Maps, North Carolina Collection, Wilson Library, University of North Carolina at Chapel Hill (Jason Tomberlin, public services librarian).